Realm 1

The Spirit's Journey

Channeled by Laura Lyn Lute

Compiled by Dale Lute

Also by Laura Lyn:

Books

- ❖ The ABC's of Psychic Development
- ❖ Healing with the Angel Rays
- ❖ Mantra's for the Soul

CD's

- ❖ Finding Your Inner Mystic - The Art of Self Discovery
- ❖ Healing with the Angel Rays Guided Meditation
- ❖ Meeting Your Angels & Spirit Guides

Oracle Cards

- ❖ Finding Your Inner Mystic

You can find all of these items at: www.angelreader.net

Copyright ©2012 by Angel Rays Publishing.

All rights reserved

No part of this publication may be reproduced, stored in a retrieval system, or transmitted in any form or by any means electronic, mechanical, photocopying, recording or otherwise without the prior permission of the author.

The medical information in this book is not intended as a substitute for consulting your physician. All matters regarding your physical health should be supervised by a medical professional. The author and publishers do not accept any responsibility for the application of any methods described in this book. The author and publisher believe this book should be available to the public for educational purposes.

Contents

Acknowledgements IX
Dedication IX
Introduction XI
About Laura Lyn XIII
Reunion with Laura - 2009 XV
About the Transcripts XIX
About the Sessions XIX
3-16-2010 1
   Meditation – Raise the Vibration 1
   Preparation for Incarnation 2
   Thank You for the Challenges 7
   The Shift 9
4-2-2010 15
   The Shift 15
   Spirit Rescue 15
   The Dead, the Undead, and the Unborn 16
   Free the Shackles 19
7-28-2010 23
   Mirror the Light 23
   There is no wrong 24
   Aligning and Balancing 25
8-29-2010 27

Helping yourself to Help Others	27
Spirit Perspective – Continued Growth	28
Communicate to Elevate	30
10-26-10	**33**
Children of the Earth	33
The Dead, the Undead and the Unborn	35
Challenges = Opportunity to Prevail	36
Prosperity Generosity	37
11-9-2010	**39**
Spirit Realm, Spirit Self	39
Helping Spirits – Selfless Help	41
11-15-2010	**45**
Healing the Earth	45
The Shift – Reincarnation – Love – Soul Groups	50
11-16-2010	**53**
Helping Spirits – Talking to Spirits	53
Earth Bound	54
1-19-2011	**59**
We are all Together	59
Prepare Yourself for the Future	62
The Earth is Alive	64
2-15- 2011	**67**
Love – The Prosperity of the Future	67
Detached Spirit –Physical Self	70

3-20-2011 ... 75
- Cleansing Mother Earth ... 75
- Simply a Thought Away - Japan Tsunami ... 76
- Spirit Realm and Human Realm are Together ... 78

3-30-2011 ... 79
- Spirit Perspective – Many Spirits ... 79
- The Heart Dwells in Light – The Shift ... 79
- Spirit Rescue ... 81
- Release and Grief ... 82
- Past Life Situation ... 82
- You are at Peace ... 84

4-4-2011 ... 87
- Unity Holds Truth for All ... 87
- Overcoming Stress ... 87
- Prayer Groups ... 89
- Love is Always the Answer ... 91

4-5-2011 ... 93
- Patterns of Life ... 93
- Shift ... 94
- Dream World – Multiple Existences ... 95
- Dream World - Counsel ... 96
- Releasing the Past ... 96
- Love Light ... 97

4-24-2011 99
See Beyond the Trees 99
Breaking the Cycle 100
Spirit Guides – Earth Angel 102
Laughter, Happiness 103
The Earth - Spirit Rescue 104
Mound Builders in Ohio 105

4-26-2011 107
Shift - Awakening 107
Glimpse of another Realm 108

5-2-2011 111
Love – Defeat Fear and Darkness 111
Beauty and Love of Oneness 112
Truth of Love 113

5-5-2011 115
Atlantis – Secrets of the Past 117
Christ Light 119

5-10-2011 121
Lost loved one 121
Embracing Love 123
Ministry – Helping 124
The Fire Keeper 125
Message from the Lumerians 126

5-11-2011 129

- Health – weight loss 131
- The Universe Depends on Mother Earth 132
- Hormones - Bioengineered foods 133
- Ascending Together 134

5-25-2011 137
- Mirror, Reflect and Internalize 137
- All is connected. All is righteous. All is truth 140
- Mirror Love 141
- Raphael - A Healing 142

6-13-2011 145
- Past Lives - Current Life Purpose 145
- Great Source of One 147

7-7-2011 151
- Remember Hearing the Spirit Within 152
- The Dead, the Undead and the Unborn 152
- Saving Lives through Sacrifice 154
- Healing from Within 158

8-9-2011 163
- Lumerians – Collision of Knowledge 163
- We Inhabit Many Dimensions 166
- Universal Life Force 167
- Bring Light to this world 168

8-14-2011 171

    It Began with Vibration 171
    What is Your Tone? 172
    Aligning with Light 174
    We are all with you 176
8-16-2011 179
    Light will Set You Free 179
    Different Planets? 180
8-19-2011 183
    Life is Love, and Love is Life 183
    You are Light 184
    Honor the Children and the Elder 185
8-23-2011 187
    Beings of Light are here 187
    Alien Beings? 189
9-18-2011 191
    All has Purpose 192
    Contagious Energy 193
    History is the Lesson 194
    Message from the Lumerians 197
9-19-2011 199
    Fighting to Become Anew 199
    Helping Yourself to Help Others 202
11-7-2011 207
    Protection – Cleansing and Sealing your space 207

- The Butterfly effect 209
- 11-21-2011 211
  - A Sum of Opportunities and Experiences 211
  - The Souls They Need Your Work 211
  - Proper Diet for Strength 212
  - Dawning a New Day 213
  - The Reason for Existence 214
  - Message from Zadkiel 215
- 12-11-2011 219
  - Aliens- Ancient Battles 219
- 1-5-2012 221
  - The New Home upon Earth 221
  - Bring Your Light 222
- 2-5-2012 223
  - Children of the Sun 223
- Summary 227

∞ *Realm to Realm* ∞

Acknowledgements

We would like to begin by acknowledging our Spirited friends. We enjoyed the love that has come through these sessions. Thank you for your powerful truths.

Please know if your name is not mentioned our heart is grateful all the same. We would like to acknowledge and thank the following...

Inspiration: Katherine Elizabeth

Transcriptions and proofing: Christy, Colette, Rebecca, Rhonda, Felicia, Courtney, Linda, Jessica

Test Readings: Jan, Jessica, Carol, Rebecca, Ben

Thank you also to all the Angel Rays for your continued support.

A special thank you to Rassouli for your wonderful art and contribution for the cover. Your gifts with color and vibration are a source of awe and inspiration.

Dedication

Mr. Cayce, I have enjoyed your books since I was very young. I will always cherish our friendship. Mr. Steiner, I regret I never heard of you before this channeling experiment. What I since learned about you has been inspiring and amazing. I am very grateful for your wise words. Thank you so much for helping my husband find his light. You have been a wonderful mentor and friend. Spotted Owl, I have known you since I was a child. I love you for all your strength and wisdom. You are a forever friend that I can't thank enough. You have helped me when I was unable to help myself. Thank you for always being there. To all the wonderful Angels and Enlightened Beings you are all astonishing. We hope this book dedicates to you the love and light that we have felt through your essence.

Dale, you are amazing and I could never express in mere words the gratitude that I have in your belief in me and in what I do. You have helped me grow so much through your deep questing. It is wonderful watching your growth; you have amazing gifts to share. The Angels brought us back together and WOW what a life we have! Thanks so much for loving me and living this crazy life (in a good way) together.

To all the brave souls who sat in for a trance channeled session, thank you for your openness. You have helped Dale and me so much. Rebecca, Ben, Jessica, Ada, Jan, we love you!

To Katherine Elizabeth, you are an amazing woman and I am sure your energy will continue to reach out to serve so many in this World who are searching for help. Thank you for finding me, I am so happy for our friendship which will continue throughout our lives.

This book is dedicated to all of you. This work is for all of us to continue to grow and search ways to share the light we have all enthusiastically enjoyed. In learning that Spirit and man alike learns and grows continually I pledge to continue questing Great Spirit and energy.

Laura Lyn

∞ Realm to Realm ∞
Introduction

My wife, Laura Lyn, has been actively communicating with spirits since she was five years old. She continues to freely speak with spirits and currently works full time as a psychic medium, speaker, and teacher.

Laura channeled all of the sessions within this book over the last two years. The hypnotic sleep trance channeled sessions book happened initially without any planning.

Here is how the sessions began. A very nice woman was in search of help because she started having psychic occurrences that were puzzling to her. She started her research at the library where she opened a book and one of Laura's cards fell out. When examining the card she felt drawn to Laura and scheduled an appointment for a reading.

Katherine Elizabeth shared with Laura about the anomalous situations that were happening. During the reading Laura was surprise to see saw Edgar Cayce with a broad smile standing behind Katherine. Laura was a big fan of Edgar Cayce so the excitement surely showed in Laura's eyes when gazing at his spirited essence.

Katherine Elizabeth was eager to learn from Edgar. It became clear there was work to be done. Katherine and Laura became fast friends and both delved in this curious experiment.

Katherine and Laura met for the first trance channel in November of 2009. Laura relaxed in a recliner and we put on some ethereal music. She went into a meditative state and after about three minutes, she began to give us beautiful messages that were much more than we expected. The session lasted about 30 minutes.

Since that first session, Laura has channeled for many friends, family, and clients. The messages have helped many to realize their potential through life path readings and past life regressions. Laura has also shared many messages in her presentations, workshops, and guided meditations.

She was invited to Columbus Ohio to speak to the Edgar Cayce's Association for Research and Enlightenment (A.R.E.), where she spoke about the messages that she has received during her channeled sessions regarding spirit perspective, healing the Earth and honoring the self through the realization of love and oneness.

∞ *Realm to Realm* ∞
About Laura Lyn

Laura is a psychic medium, paranormal investigator, teacher and author; who works primarily with Angels, Spirits and Guides. She first began having experiences with Angels and Spirits as a small child. In her early twenties she decided to pursue working with these enlightened beings as a career to help others in their search for healing and enlightenment.

Laura's focus is to bring forth the awareness of healing through love, while teaching many how to open up to their own spiritual potential. She has published two books, *The ABC's of Psychic Development* and *Healing with the Angel Rays*. She also holds classes and workshops nationwide that allow the individual to open up to the spiritual realm.

Laura teaches Angel Ray classes at Lily Dale in New York and has exceeded the attendance records for her powerful *"Ask the Psychic"* presentations held at the Cuyahoga Falls Library. She has also held similar events at Kent State University. Laura helps to raise funds for the Summit County Historical Society through her quarterly *"Realm to Realm"* events at the Perkins Mansion in Akron, Ohio.

In order to reach a larger audience, Laura founded The Angel Rays Enrichment Center in Cuyahoga Falls, Ohio. The mission statement for the center is, *"as a Spiritual Enrichment Center we embrace the great truth of Oneness; finding freedom through self-realization of body, mind and soul."* The center is focused on a community, where love is

∞ *About Laura Lyn* ∞

always the answer. Laura believes that Spirit is everywhere and lives in the heart and soul of every being.

The Angel Rays Enrichment Center holds Sunday gatherings centered on the book, *Mantras for the Soul*, which is based on the works of Rudolf Steiner. This book was co-authored by Laura Lyn and her husband, Dale Lute. The get-togethers focus on bringing forth oneness of mind, body and soul through weekly mantras, music and meditation.

As a teacher and paranormal investigator for S.I.G.H.T. (Spiritual Insight Ghost Hunting Team), Laura Lyn has taught classes to hundreds of individuals, sharing her knowledge of the spiritual methods of ghost hunting. In these classes she explains that ghosts are people who have passed from our physical realm and into the spiritual realm and teaches that they should be treated with honor and respect. Laura aids in spirit rescue and cleansings, where she helps to bring peace to both the physical and spiritual beings that are in distress.

∞ Realm to Realm ∞
Reunion with Laura - 2009

While in high school, I dated a girl for part of my senior year. My parents would drop me off at her house on the weekends. We would spend hours on the loveseat in her parent's living room, sneaking a kiss when we were alone. We took walks in the woods by her house and enjoyed spending time together.

There was something special about her. At seventeen years old I didn't have the insight to understand what it was. We both had troubled childhoods which caused us to move to different parts of the country. We wrote letters for a while but lost track of each other. I married someone else about two years later.

Almost thirty years had passed. I had been drinking heavily for about twelve years. Life seemed to be a punishment. I felt trapped and I wanted it all to end. I regularly envisioned driving my car off a cliff or into a wall just to get it over with.

By 2009, I was a travelling computer technician. My work kept me on the road at least three weeks a month. One night I was sitting alone in a hotel room checking my Facebook and getting ready to drink myself to sleep, when I received a message from Laura Lyn.

She wrote that she was happy to see (from my online profile) that I was doing well, and she was sorry for any trouble she may have caused me in the past. She told me that I may think she's odd, but she was a full time psychic medium.

∞ Reunion with Laura 2009 ∞

I didn't believe in any of that "psychic stuff" I was an absolute non believer. I had no problem with what others thought or did, but psychic abilities seemed to be fabricated nonsense to me. I had no idea that things were about to change.

I wanted to call her to let her know that she had never caused me any trouble in the past. I quickly found Laura's phone number online and went outside to call her.

She was in a meeting but stepped out to talk with me for a minute. We reminisced for a while and I assured her that I was never angry with her over anything from the past.

Laura asked about how my life was going. I told her that everything she saw online was not the truth. I was a very unhappy drunk. We talked for about twenty minutes and decided that we would continue the conversation after her meeting. She called me back about an hour later and we reminisced a little more.

As I hung up the phone I realized that Laura and I had never broken up. She got sent away and I ended up living in Florida. Things just got messed up. What had I done? As I walked back to my hotel room, everything about my life became clear. What had I been doing these past 30 years? There was no sleep for me that night.

On the eight hour trip home the next day, I thought about my life and tried to figure out what had gone wrong. My thoughts kept drifting back to Laura. I had to see her.

We met two days later. (It was completely my idea.) Laura and I happened to live within two miles of each other. We talked about everything that we had been through over the years. We quickly got reacquainted and become close friends. Within five months, we moved in to our home together.

I had an immediate spiritual awakening after the reunion with Laura. Up to that point I was a complete Atheist. I was in a very dark place but immediately life became very vibrant and alive. My job required me to be out of town most of the time for the six months after speaking with Laura.

The contrast from the dark to the light was apparent to everyone. My nights of drinking myself to sleep and agonizing over life were over. My new craving became learning about love. The Metaphysical books and studies throughout the last few years (since June 17, 2009) served me well to release the anguish and pain.

We are now happily married. February 18th is my wife's birthday and our wedding anniversary.

Thank you for finding me again Laura,

Dale

∞ *Reunion with Laura 2009* ∞

About the Transcripts

I resisted editing the channeled messages in this book because I felt that it was not my place to change anything that is spoken by spirits and enlightened beings. I would honor the word of spirit no matter what.

I spent over a year reading and contemplating these transcripts before I began to share them with friends. I found that some of the messages were difficult for others to follow. They seemed fine to me because I had read them many times and became accustomed to the way the information was conveyed.

In order to clarify the channeled messages I have removed repeated words and did my best with punctuation. Footnotes are included at the *end* of each session in order to keep things clear.

Some personal information was removed in order to respect the privacy of our friends. I have made every effort to honor the original messages and keep them intact and exact.

About the Sessions

It may be helpful for you to take the session's one at a time slowly and meditate after each to see what is revealed to you through Spirit. We believe everyone has the ability to hear Spirit with a little patience and practice.

While in a sleep state, Laura has connected with many spirits that we feel have become our dear friends. Each session is listed by date and who came through. While I asked for assistance with personal growth, I also asked for global messages.

Within this book you will find universal guidance that we hope will help many on their life path. While everybody has different paths and journeys it is our hope you can glean the similarities that are taking place in your life.

We hope your belief and understanding in your Spiritual Counsel is increased from the words in this book. We have no doubt every person living on this great Earth has their own counsel (guides, guardians, ancestors, masters, loved ones...) that helps the individual through the spirit presence and physical existence.

Above all enjoy the possibilities! Remember I was a complete non believer until June 17, 2009. I am now a complete believer that all is possible through love and light.

Dale Lute

∞ Realm to Realm ∞

The Sessions

March 16, 2010

To

March 4, 2012

∞ Realm to Realm ∞
3-16-2010
Yogananda, Edgar Cayce, Chief Wolf
∞

This is one of the early sessions that Laura channeled. We had a friend stop by to ask questions about spiritual growth and reincarnation. At this time it was still a fairly new experience for all of us.

Dale: Who are we speaking with?

Laura Lyn: We have present three major energies. Yogananda[1] is here present who will bring wisdom and enlightenment. Edgar Cayce[2] is here present who will bring information on medical and prophet information forward, prophecy for a new world. And then we have Chief Wolf[3] present who will bring forward life path information.

Meditation – Raise the Vibration

Guest: I have been going through some major changes recently. I have an increased awareness that seemed to come from nowhere. Can you explain the ringing in my ears?

Laura Lyn: What you are hearing is alignment with a higher vibration. There are people who are hearing this through the shimmering in their ears and feeling it through electrical pulse points throughout their meridian system in their body. You are systematically working throughout the system the electrical charges which are aligning to the higher vibration in the atmosphere.

Guest: What else would help open my channel and raise my vibration?

Laura Lyn: Meditation[4] is the most powerful way to open that channel.

Guest: What kind of meditation?

Laura Lyn: Allowing just simple relaxation in the night time hours and opening up the third eye,[5] allowing the color blue to flow through to open up the space and just be, just simply be.

There is no action necessary; just rest while going into that sleep realm.[6] You will be communicating with many spirits that will bring inspiration. In the morning you will be inspired to write. Allow the energies to flow accordingly.

Guest: Should I ask specific questions before I go to sleep?

Laura Lyn: Yes, you may ask specific questions and allow your dream world to receive the answers. Your subconscious (higher self) will capture it and you will have the information stored for when it is necessary to come forward and be revealed.

Preparation for Incarnation

Guest: If a spirit is preparing to come back and have another physical experience on earth, what is it like to plan your next experience? Would it be possible to make an educated decision while in spirit realm?

Laura Lyn: It is like watching it on a screen. Imagine watching a movie on a screen in your mind's eye. The difference is, you are within this movie and you are feeling the drama, you are actually feeling the energy.

Yes there is unconditional love in that sphere[7], but that love is helping the informer to make decisions on the life that will help bring forward knowledge. Everyone's decision on the life path present has been felt and will be felt with the decision made.

When you are seeing the act of your life time in the future, you are feeling the energy within the heart sphere. So therefore, you are in touch with it through your feeling, thought pattern, and energetically. Being embraced by the energy, you are bringing forward your knowledge for your future.

So yes, you are informed. We also have a degree of change that can become part of the life through choice. With this knowledge and act, become aware that people can change their routes, their decisions, their roads, and their destiny. So therefore, it is two-fold protection before the person is born and after they are born. The contract can be changed.

Guest: What else can you tell me about planning another physical experience on earth? What are some important things I should know or understand about reincarnation?

Laura Lyn: Planning your next physical life is one process. There are many more layers that happen before this planning takes place. This is a Hindan[8] inspired process. We brought forward this knowledge to the Hindu's. There are so many layers that take place previous to the planning such as: the resolution of life, feeling the highest

potentials of joy, the frequencies of harmony, and the complete information of the unconditional sphere of love. You're bathed in that love within that process.

This is the nirvana that we speak of that can be actualized. The layers of this frequency are what people are going toward from the shift and we are hoping that people stay in that sphere; to grow in that sphere of the unconditional love so that the reincarnation doesn't need to take place. Once you get into that state, to nirvana, you can evaporate into all that energy and be one with the creator.

Guest: Why wouldn't reincarnation need to take place or not need to take place?

Laura Lyn: Because once you are highest elevated, another birth no longer needs to take place.

Guest: For people who do not want to incarnate again what can they do in their current lifetime so they don't need to come back.

Laura Lyn: It's not a choice. It is only after the lessons are learned and the truth state that we were speaking of can take place and that nirvana is realized. It is a decision though, it is a decision to live your life of purity and love and unselfishness and that is the lessons that Yogananda speaks of.

Guest: If someone is born into a family in which their parents are abusive, did the spirit or soul choose that consciously with the parent? Was it possibly just an energetic or vibrational connection that drew them together automatically?

Laura Lyn: When a person is drawn to an abusive situation, it is karmic effect. What happens when people are being drawn to parents or family is the situation is drawn where the family knows the soul pattern. The soul group [9]energetically goes where they need to go in order to learn a lesson. So therefore, the decision is made as a soul group.

Guest: If someone who's in physical form decided to change their life so that there was going to be less suffering, but had not learned the lessons, would they be able to change it?

Laura Lyn: Yes, they could. They would just decide to change the route of how long the lesson would take to be learned. We have new opportunities with each life change, with each life pattern. Several life changes can come on simultaneously that would allow this embracement to happen.

Guest: What is affected by changing your current life?

Laura Lyn: We are in a place electronically, energetically, through our electric system, through our brain, and our heart, that our patterns are being felt simultaneously. So therefore, in addition to the life pattern that you have the knowledge of at this moment, you are also working on another lifetime in a distant place which is here in this frequency.

In actuality there are several life time spans that you are working through in a simultaneous manner that allow all of this to take place.

∞ The Spirit's Journey ∞

Guest: If someone wanted to completely change their life plan how would they do that?

Laura Lyn: They would make a decision based on their life to make a change that would alter the existence such as divorce, moving, travel, manifestation, changing careers, or changing opportunities. It is that simple.

Guest: Is there an absolutely set plan for our lives?

Laura Lyn: No, that's where miracles come into play. And miracles are those joyous, serendipitous moments that allow life to be so joyous and free. That is an evolution.

Guest: Is it fair to make a drastic change in your life path? Could you miss lessons that are needed?

Laura Lyn: The life pattern, the physical self, if you will, is the lower vibration of the higher self[10]. The physical self is the one who brings forward the lessons and truths so the higher self can evaluate and express forward, move forward to a higher level and energy; therefore the physical self expects and understands that this is not about fairness this is about truth.

This physical self can explore life and feel great joy. The higher self can feel unconditional love but cannot feel the ultimate joy of the earthen body. Therefore there is truth in both the higher self and the physical self that must be met.

Guest: What can I do to reach my highest potential?

Laura Lyn: Allow yourself and your cause to come through and flow. When you are ready, bring your cause forward; you can open up yourself to the world for highest

∞ Realm to Realm ∞

potentials for growth. Reap in your heart where that cause is, and open up your world for potentials to grow and allow the resources to move forward.

Thank You for the Challenges

Guest: Why are there so many challenges that cause suffering? Wasn't the original plan for earth that people would learn just through love and joy?

Laura Lyn: Agreed, the reason for all the focus on challenges is that this is where the earthen body lays, in challenges. The shift[11] will help reveal the highest light, highest glory, and that joy and love. That is what is being learned.

Guest: How can I help people who have experienced trauma? What will help them to heal?

Laura Lyn: Healing takes place when one accepts the healing internally. This is an internal work that comes forward sometimes through miraculous means. It's essentially an internal exercise that must be met inside with the act of living and acknowledging the God within. This is critical for the change and the healing to take place.

Guest: You mentioned that people have to accept the healing. Everyone who's trying to heal has as intent to accept the healing. No one is saying I don't want this healing. But a lot of those people still don't heal. So what does it mean, how do people accept healing?

Laura Lyn: They bring the knowledge forward that they are already healed, whole and complete. The physical challenges are a mirage. If the person has no legs they can

∞ *The Spirit's Journey* ∞

still walk. That sounds preposterous but yet it's true. The challenges are in a physical sense, getting beyond that in the internal high knowledge, understanding that the illusion is set forward to present these challenges. We are aware that we can become inspired to go beyond the limitations, and that is where the truth of God reveals that all is love. Once you embrace that knowledge of total love you are in that existence of healing.

Guest: I notice that a lot of people say that they've gone through some kind of trauma. They say that they need emotional healing, and they say they don't know what that means or how to go about it. What would you say about that?

Laura Lyn: We know that the one channeling the messages, Laura, received the knowledge that the rays of light[12] that are the frequencies of the highest consciousness of love and truth have been, and will always be within her. Therefore, she became grateful for the experiences that she had taken in the past. This helped her move forward to become an advocate for others that also present these challenges[13].

This is an example of how a deep healing can take place. With this, healing and release will take place. The release will help forget the past pain, and also remember the past with deep gratitude for the experience. This can take place by merely asking for the healing and saying thank you for the challenges.

Guest: What about for people who are still lost in the trauma and want emotional healing. What can they do to heal?

Laura Lyn: If they find the healers that can help them find that place, they will get there. Find a way to bring forward the resources to help the people get to the proper places that they may be led to go to, even when money may be a challenge.

The Shift

Laura Lyn: We are here to explain there is a new order coming. This has been prophesized in the distance. This order will help bring forward resurrection and truth for all. It will also bring fear for many. This one world truth is intended to help bring forward oneness. The ideal of oneness[14] has been prophesized. With this one order, truth will be established. Religion and dogma will be erased, and within a century this world will be none like you see today. Harmony and peace will prevail.

Know that the tides are shifting and the winds are drifting forward to a direction and a source that is pure love and pure light. Spread the knowledge forward that will help bring the peace and harmony that is so needed in the land that will restore the harmony to Mother Earth. Thank you for bringing the question forward.

Guest: The shifts that you're talking about, will something major happen in 2012?

Laura Lyn: It is already happening, it is already taking place. There will be earthquakes trembling, there will be fires, there will be floods, but this is a natural reaction from the damage that has taken place on Mother Earth.

There will be lives lost but this has already happened and, will continue happening. The shift that has been

earmarked for 2012 is continuing and will continue beyond that point.

Dale: Is there anything else you would like to tell us before I wake Laura?

Laura Lyn: We are grateful that we can speak and bring forward messages of hope and love. We encourage you to listen and realize that we have a unique perspective. We are hopeful that your life will be complete; full of love and honor. We thank you for being here.

Dale: I would like to thank you for being here as well. And also I would like to ask that you help Laura come back to us now if you can. I am asking her guides, angels if they can help her come back to us. We are done with our questions.

---

[1] YogaNanda - (born January 5, 1893 – died March 7, 1952) - was an Indian yogi and guru who introduced many westerners to the teachings of meditation and Kriya Yoga through his book, Autobiography of a Yogi.

[2] Edgar Cayce - (born March 18, 1877 – died January 3, 1945) - was an American psychic who allegedly had the ability to give answers to questions on subjects such as healing or Atlantis while in a hypnotic trance. Though Cayce himself was a devout Christian and lived before the emergence of the New Age Movement, some believe he was the founder of the movement and influenced its teachings.

[3] Chief Wolf – A Native American enlightened being and Spirit Guide.

[4] Meditation - is any form of a family of practices in which practitioners train their minds or self-induce a mode of consciousness to realize some benefit.

[5] Third Eye - The third eye (also known as the inner eye) is a mystical and esoteric concept referring in part to the ajna (brow) chakra in certain dharmic spiritual traditions, in particular Hinduism. This concept was later adopted by Christian mystics and spiritualists as well as people from other religious faiths. It is also spoken of as the gate that leads within to inner realms and spaces of higher consciousness.

[6] Sleep Realm – (Also called Dream World) When in a deep sleep state, many believe that what goes on in your dreams is actually happening in another realm of consciousness. Some feel that we are actually living within the realm of spirit when we are dreaming.

[7] Sphere - What we would think of as realms or dimensions are referred to as sphere throughout the channeled messages.

[8] Reincarnation - Hindan inspired process is referring to Reincarnation which best describes the concept where the soul or spirit, after the death of the body, is believed to return to live in a new human body, or, in some

∞ The Spirit's Journey ∞

traditions, either as a human being, animal or plant. This doctrine is a central tenet within the majority of Indian religious traditions, such as Hinduism, Jainism, and Sikhism; the Buddhist concept of rebirth is also often referred to as reincarnation.

[9] Soul Group - Any number of souls that tend to reincarnate within the same time and space. It is very likely that those within your current circle of family and friends are part of a soul group.

[10] Higher Self - is a new age term associated with multiple belief systems, but its basic premise describes an eternal, omnipotent, conscious, and intelligent being, who is one's real self.

[11] The Shift - A stage which marks a period in which Earth and its inhabitants may undergo a positive physical or spiritual transformation, and that 2012 may mark the beginning of a new era. Others suggest that the 2012 date marks the end of the world or a similar catastrophe.

[12] Rays of Light - Refers to Angel Rays, which are various colors of light which represent angelic frequencies. This is how Laura Lyn has interpreted Angels throughout her life. More details can be found in her book: *Healing with the Angel Rays*.

[13] Laura's advocate work - Laura Lyn worked at the Mental Health Association and many advocacy groups

across the state of Ohio. She worked with legislators to help children with mental health diagnosis receive rights in schools.

[14] Oneness – The concept in which all is connected. Oneness is discussed throughout this book.

∞ *The Spirit's Journey* ∞

∞ *Realm to Realm* ∞

4-2-2010

Edgar Cayce, Rudolf Steiner, Carl Jung, Spotted Owl

∞

This session was just Laura and I. Spirit rescue is discussed and explained in this session. During this time, I was just beginning to study the work of Rudolf Steiner[1].

Dale: Who am I speaking with right now?

Laura Lyn: We have four with us right now. Edgar Cayce, Rudolph Steiner, Carl Jung[2] and we have Spotted Owl[3].

The Shift

Dale: (*To Rudolf Steiner)* which of your works should I study? Am I reading the right books?

Laura Lyn: You are bringing forth the information that I would like to share with the modern world. This will help the truth to align to a flow of energy that has a frequency of light that needed to be expressed over two hundred years ago. The truth is that we are behind times and the new truth, the new thought is finally expressing and real.

Spirit Rescue

Dale: (T*o Carl Jung*) Laura channeled that I should read your book: *The Red Book*[4]. I became very sad while reading the first few chapters. Do I need to read the entire Red Book to understand the messages?

Laura Lyn: No Dale, you are receiving the messages rapidly. I'm sorry that I took you down a road that few have travelled. That darkness and sadness that you were

∞ The Spirit's Journey ∞

feeling, and taken upon yourself, I have journeyed for years. I have travelled down that road that men have not travelled frequently; I was taking on that misled mismarked formation of what some call sin just as Christ has taken on.

Living in hell; living in that place of despair; I was taking on and sacrificing so that others would not need to. There is a deep dark truth resounding in this text. Part of your job (*part of the job*), is to bring forward information regarding the abilities that we are tapping into.

This information must and needs to be used to release the souls that are in this dreaded pathway of confusion. Christ, the true Christ, never intended for people to remain in this quandary where they are now lost, looking, searching.

There are many dead souls looking for rapture[5] that will never take place. We are speaking truth that these souls must be unshackled and the fears released so that the truth of freedom and light remains. This truth will allow these souls to walk through that doorway of light. Here is the answer: to free the dimensions of many.

Dale: You are speaking of spirit rescue?

Laura Lyn: Yes. That is correct

The Dead, the Undead, and the Unborn

Dale: Is the chaos in the physical world affecting your world? And spirit rescue will help all realms?

Laura Lyn: Yes. There are three realms that are directly affected. We are affecting the realm of the dead, the undead and the unborn[6]. The unborn of the future are waiting for the dead to receive the light so they can come into this sphere. The unborn, the souls that will take place and harbor their step and beauty on this earth cannot and will not take their step until the dead, the earthen dead, are released into the light.

Dale: I have found that energy and our thoughts are contagious. Is it the same? Is spirit rescue something that can pass along and help many?

Laura Lyn: Yes it does. A great light shines. There are many souls that you are unaware of that are in line for this truth. A great cathedral opens its doorways when we speak of love and enlightenment. There are many that follow you home to hear the message.

When Laura is speaking of love and truth, she understands that these spirits are here. They talk to her endlessly. They hear her light; they see her light. She is helping them even in her sleep. She has freed thousands upon thousands of souls, and her job will never end because she fearlessly helps discover the light for these souls.

This calling which she has taken upon herself has actually helped this world as you know it also. She is helping the dead, the undead, and the unborn of the future. So it happens in threes, that powerful number three, that she speaks of. That is where the power is; in the three dimensions.

Dale: What can I do to help Laura?

Laura Lyn: You are helping Laura by relieving the tasks that she has found difficult. She works freely with spirit. Subconsciously, consciously, in her awakened, and her sleeping state. She cannot help but to help. Her life is to help. That is her cause and her mission.

All she knows is to help. This is her life and journey and if you will, even her sacrifice. However, it is necessary and truth does prevail. She will be fine. This is her journey and her path. She will continue this work because she has to continue this work.

Spiritual Awakening

Dale: I had an awakening[7] when Laura and I were reacquainted. We had been apart for thirty years. I was in a state of joy and pure realization that I had never felt before. Now I find that my past thought patterns keep coming back to haunt me. How can I get back there? It's where I want to be.

Laura Lyn: You are in the glimpse of it today. You have felt it have you not?[8] You are receiving it, and it is coming back rapidly. You've had to release the emotions from the past 27 years of your life. So that takes time.

But today is a new day and you are feeling that energy, and that wonderful relief of the light; and this filtered light that's coming forward will help you embrace the truth of who you are. You are that of spirit; that of helping people move forward in their lives.

We remember watching you when you felt uncomfortable with the spirit rescue process. We chuckled and laughed and thought it was great interest that you had thought that the spirit was untruth but now you see the truth. You are a spirit rescue resource.

We weren't laughing at you Dale, we love you dearly. We feel that you are here for a great purpose to help great men and women find their place through that doorway.

Free the Shackles

Dale: Is there anything else that you would like to say to the world?

This work (spirit rescue) will help free the shackles because a new truth of bringing honor to helping others will be the new story of the land. To not look inside but outside, selflessness, not an ego driven place, but a selfless place[9]. This will bring forward the frequency of truth of helping yourself to help others. Allow that energy to come forward to bless man and bless woman.

Dale: Thank You.

Perfection – Higher Love

Laura Lyn: Thank you Dale, and Dale, we have a message for you. You are a beautiful soul. You have felt great pain, great confusion and sadness in your life and we are aware that you have come to the depths, the depths of pain, and what you are looking for is perfection in your life.

Perfection comes through in one universal flow of love. The love that we are speaking of is a higher love. It doesn't come from things, or capital. It comes from a source that you are now tapping into: God. God is real; God is all around you. The huge wonderful energy of God surrounds you. Tapping into that source, you will live your life completely fulfilled, joyful, and free, and we hope that you can tap into this world with love; love being at the foot and the crown. We are loving you and thanking you for being here.

Dale: I'm trying very hard to reach my heightened self...I think I just have habitual thoughts that I'm trying to get rid of.

Laura Lyn: Release them. Just let them go. They're not important. What's important is helping and freeing. And as you free more, you will free.

---

[1] Rudolf Steiner - Rudolf Joseph Lorenz Steiner (Born - 25/27 February 1861 - 30 Died - March 1925) was an Austrian philosopher, social reformer, architect, and esotericist. He gained initial recognition as a literary critic and cultural philosopher. At the beginning of the 20th century, he founded a spiritual movement, Anthroposophy, as an esoteric philosophy growing out of European transcendentalism and with links to Theosophy.

[2] Carl Jung - Carl Gustav Jung (Born - 26 July 1875 - Died - 6 June 1961) was a Swiss psychiatrist and the founder of analytical psychology. Jung is considered the first modern psychiatrist to view the human psyche as "by nature religious" and make it the focus of exploration.[1] Jung is one of the best known researchers in the field of dream analysis and symbolization. While he was a fully involved and practicing clinician, much of his life's work was spent exploring tangential areas, including Eastern and Western philosophy, alchemy, astrology, and sociology, as well as literature and the arts.

[3] Spotted Owl - Laura's Native American Spirit Guide.

[4] Red Book - *A few weeks before this session, Laura channeled that we should research two books. One of the books she mentioned was The Red Book. The other book was called The Golden Key. Neither of us had heard of*

these books. I got online and started searching and found a description on Wikipedia:

The Red Book, also known as Liber Novus (Latin for New Book), is a 205-page manuscript written and illustrated by Swiss psychiatrist Carl Gustav Jung between approximately 1914 and 1930, prepared for publication on October 7, 2009. Until 2001, his heirs denied scholars access to the book, which he began after a falling-out with Sigmund Freud in 1913.

Carl Jung originally titled the manuscript Liber Novus (literally meaning A New Book in Latin), but it was informally known and published as The Red Book. The book is written in calligraphic text and contains many illuminations.

[5] Rapture - The state of being transported by a lofty emotion; ecstasy, An expression of ecstatic feeling. Often used in the plural, The transporting of a person from one place to another, especially to heaven.

[6] The dead, the undead, and the unborn – we in the physical are the undead. The dead are those who are lost in a realm through fear, sadness, regret; lost without seeing the light, lost in the darkness. The unborn are those who are seeking to return to a physical state in order to learn and round out their being.

[7] Awakening (Spiritual) - Religious experience (sometimes known as a spiritual experience, sacred experience, or mystical experience) is a subjective experience where an individual reports contact with a transcendent reality, an encounter or union with the divine.

[8] You are in a glimpse of it today – *I was also studying The Golden Key by written by Emmet Fox. This work was giving me a new insight on dealing with the stresses in life. The book can be summarized with one line: Stop thinking about the difficulty, whatever it is, and think about God instead.*

[9] Selflessness - the quality of not putting yourself first but being willing to give your time or effort etc. This is one aspect of the shift.

∞ *The Spirit's Journey* ∞

∞ Realm to Realm ∞
7-28-2010
Spotted Owl, Edgar Cayce, Rudolf Steiner
∞

Laura Lyn: I am asking that only the highest greatest good can come forward and that those who we are channeling come forward very clearly and distinctly. I am asking that we are guided and the question's that Dale asks come from a place of love and honor so that we can work with spirit in a way that is of the path of the greatest good and on the path to help betterment of man.

We are saying thank you, thank you Archangel Michael for your protection. And I am asking guidance to come forward, the spirits, spirit guides, and enlightened beings. I would like the counsel to come forward to speak.

Dale: Could you tell me who's with us tonight?

Laura Lyn: I am seeing three. Who are you please? As I gently go to sleep please talk through me. I have Spotted Owl, Edgar Cayce and Rudolph Steiner.

Mirror the Light

Dale: What it the best way to handle forceful or aggressive people?

Laura Lyn: It is natural to have those within families and groups. They have a difficult time with socialization and particularly with people who are attempting to raise their vibration who are also at a place of inner insecurity. These people may not appear insecure in their outer being, yet their inner spirit is immature and young.

Allow the wisdom that flows to be mirrored to show a better way. Do not attempt to block them but help them rise. You then have a unique opportunity to help these young ones to grow, to strengthen, and be a powerful voice for spirit.

Yet if you allow that immature voice to interfere with the greater picture it could have devastating results. So we ask you to bring balance. We ask you to be forthright in what you are attempting to deliver for spirit.

Do not allow people to interfere with the goal of helping those people who desperately need to be risen, to rise. Those souls that are ready to come forward into the dimension of the here and now experience on planet earth at this moment cannot come forward if they do not have someone who is able and willing to help them through that void.

This is the picture, this is the place, this is the opportunity that will open and rise. Many will be saved and harbored through. You will have an opportunity to help.

Do not allow the distractions to stop this process. Help the people that you speak of to rise to the occasion so that they too can have a part in raising their vibration.

There is no wrong

Dale: It is very difficult for me to find a way to relay the message without telling someone that imposing upon others is wrong. How could one do that gently?

Laura Lyn: There is no wrong or right in this process. Everybody's path is their own. What you perceive as wrong is only a lesson, a lesson for your heart and your spirit to take through and take in.

Dale: If someone is full of self-doubt and asking for help; how do you help them without criticism? Is it just through example; is that the best way to handle this?

Laura Lyn: Yes, through example and also by using the code that Laura teaches readily. They were delivered to her for a reason and a purpose. That for the greatest good, that for the greatest light, that for the greatest love that is a powerful prayer. Use it often, utilize this as a mantra. For everybody that has any ability to bring forward a lower vibration utilize this prayer readily and you will see a change take place promptly and swiftly.

Aligning and Balancing

Dale: Is there anything else you would like to relay to us before I bring Laura back?

Laura Lyn: We want to reiterate the importance of helping the tears and sorrow that need to be lifted and released from these groups of souls that are trapped.

There is an outer world and an inner world that you are working through. Sometimes you can barely and subtly distinguish these worlds. There are three worlds that you are tapping into at any time. Information flows through these three worlds at a frequency that is either a little higher or a little below the frequency you are tuned in to now.

The grids that are forming on this earth are aligning and they amplify the frequency so that these subtle changes are becoming more amplified and direct. Allow this energy to

∞ *The Spirit's Journey* ∞

move forward through you, multiplying and balancing. You will feel and see the energies being formed.

The delicate system within is moving at an enhanced rate. You will see and hear the frequencies within your ears as the grids align. Open your heart space for this and you will be filled. You will be filled with a love that is unconditional, powerful and old. We thank you for speaking with us tonight.

Dale: And I thank you. And I would like to ask that Edgar, Rudolph and Spotted Owl help bring Laura back here with me. I am asking her guides and the angels to help wake her. Thank you.

Laura Lyn: Thank you.

∞ Realm to Realm ∞
8-29-2010
Edgar Cayce, Spotted Owl
∞

This session is the first session that Laura and I did with the idea of gathering information for this book. I asked a couple questions regarding the book and I asked questions about spirit existence. There are references to helping those who are in prisons and institutions. At this time, Laura had given talks in prisons three times. Laura has done much work to help mentally disabled children through advocacy work. Some of this work is referred to here.

Dale: Who's with us this evening?

Laura Lyn: There are many spirits present. We are eager for your query.

Helping yourself to Help Others

Dale: Thank you. Are there any specific details that you can share with us about our work?

Laura Lyn: Yes, there is. The work will help many children and many families. We will prepare the words through Laura for a channeled message for those who unfortunately find themselves in a place of solitude or a place where they are in a prison or institution[1].

We fully suspect this meditation and art to help bring healing to a population that badly needs the energy raised. This is a great spirit, a great movement that will help reduce violence and enraged personal defeat. We are looking to help the prisoners to get to a place of peace within, and as that energy elevates, the whole energy from a universal stance will also elevate.

There is another area that Laura finds very dear and this area has to do with children that have special unique abilities. You see these children have the ability to look and see right through the universe, to capture the essence that we carry.[2]

The unfortunate difficulty is that most people walking upon the earth do not understand these children. Please listen to the guidance that Laura shares for this is a beautiful vision. The children they need art. The children need to be inspired within and once they capture that light they can move forward in a place of peace and love.

What we are looking for is the dear ones to find the love in their heart so they want to move forward and help others. That has always been the message to carry forward.

Once you help others you can always help yourself. Help yourself and you are helping others. It goes in a magical way. These children are seeking that self-expression and if the children are allowed, they will be honored to bring forward their magic to help the land.

Everyone should know and carry through their life knowing that they are loved deeply. Everyone on this earth is unique, honored and loved. Believe in this and know that it is true. We honor you and we thank you.

Spirit Perspective – Continued Growth

Dale: What happens after we pass? Do we continue to learn and grow as individuals?

Laura Lyn: In spirit world you are continually evolving. The thought pattern will move forward in many directions. You have upon yourself, in spirit world, the foundation of knowledge that is never ceasing never ending. You are evolving to the perfect performance of your potential that you received here on earth.

Here on earth, the purpose is to elevate, to find that love is the perfection within and without, all through the senses; if you understand that love is the direction and movement.

When you move to the other point of existence, which you may call a realm[3], you search knowledge and you evolve accordingly. The patterns of thought never cease, never end, however, thought is erroneous. What happens is that your perfect instinct is to elevate, and within that elevation moment, if you would want to call this place the enlightened state[4], you are evolving to higher places for this is the manifestation of truth.

What we are seeking and looking for as humans is to move forward in that elevation of truth. We are here to honor those who are seeking truth and to help them through that enlightened state.

For those that are deciding to go into a different direction; they are seeking what we would refer to as darkness[5] for they are in their own anger. Those cells, we call them cells, are within their own self and cannot project forward. Unfortunately, the cells stay on the earth. And those cells have an opportunity to hurt earthen beings. The earthen beings are either weakened or strong. The strength is

∞ *The Spirit's Journey* ∞

within themselves when they feel the spirit. We welcome more questions.

Dale: How we can help these "cells"?

Communicate to Elevate

Laura Lyn: We ask you, and encourage you, to communicate with them, to talk with them. They can hear you. They are here all over the earth, they are among you everywhere. You really can't shield yourself from them. Sometimes people will call these cells orbs, orbs of light.

What they really are is consciousness that is seeking a direction of truth.

Where there is happiness these orbs will be there looking for that light. They are there to find that light and inspiration. They seem to congregate around enlightened beings. They seem to congregate around people. They are looking for, and searching for truth.

These cells, these single cells are looking for a new direction. Communicate with them often and they will elevate. These single cells are able to communicate for that consciousness of thought is still within them. When they seek help or direction, be there to help counsel them into that place of light.

Earthly Distraction

Dale: Is there a major change that happens when a person dies? Do you still stay who you are?

Laura Lyn: You do stay who you are but your self can greatly increase the frequency very rapidly without the earthly distractions and responsibilities. Your body elevates

∞ *Realm to Realm* ∞

to a point of perfection in a rapid sense. We ask you to understand that in this realm here now, your life has so many distractions on a day to day basis that it is impossible to elevate to that place of perfection unless you are in a cave, or in a place of solitude. You have so many energies pulling you down that your body can't possibly become enfolded into the perfected self that your wisdom self is seeking.

You do go in the other realms as yourself, but rapidly changing. You cease to seek that knowledge that you are wanting to obtain to elevate.

Your self is within the perfect opportunity to seek that perfect light and that wisdom. The wisdom makers will come forward to bring solutions to the grounded earth people. That is what you refer to as guides.

We are asking you to awaken Laura for she is at a place now that is going to be very depleting.

---

[1] The work that is mentioned here is the work that Laura does with the prisons. She has performed guided meditations as part of the presentations at the prisons. More on this work can be found in Carol's session dated 3-7-2011

[2] Crystal children, Star children Indigo children- Descriptions of indigo children include the belief that they are empathetic, curious, strong-willed, independent, and often perceived by friends and family as being strange; possess a clear sense of self-definition and purpose; and also exhibit a strong innate sub-conscious spirituality from early childhood (which, however, does not necessarily imply a direct interest in spiritual or religious areas). Other alleged traits include a high

intelligence quotient, an inherent intuitive ability, and resistance to rigid, control-based paradigms of authority.

[3] Realm - the region, sphere, or domain within which something or someone exists, acts, or has influence or power.

[4] Enlightened state - in a secular context often means the "full comprehension of a situation", but in spiritual terms the word alludes to a spiritual revelation or deep insight into the meaning and purpose of all things, communication with or understanding of the mind of God, profound spiritual understanding or a fundamentally changed consciousness whereby everything is perceived as a unity.

[5] Darkness - lack of knowledge or enlightenment, obscurity; concealment.

∞ Realm to Realm ∞
10-26-10
Edgar Cayce, Spotted Owl
∞

Laura Lyn: We are asking the enlightened beings to help bring forward a message for the greatest good of all. We're asking that this protection encircles each and every one of us so that we're on our journey to help bring in that beautiful energy of the highest greatest good. We're asking that consciousness of love to unfold the room and for us to be at a place of peace during this journey.

I'm asking my guides and Angels to come forward, my counsel to come forward to speak through me while I'm asleep. Help bring the messages of the future journey to help serve with honor. Thank you spirit guides and messengers for being here. I'm asking my guidance to help me fall into that trance state where I can be safely guarded while the enlightened beings are working through me. We are here and welcome. Thank you.

Dale: Who is with us this evening?

Laura Lyn: Edgar Cayce is present along with Spotted Owl.

Children of the Earth

Dale: Is there a general message that you have for us tonight?

Laura Lyn: You are all children of the earth. Your presence is here to heal. As you are walking upon the earth, know that you bring forward your strength and

∞ *The Spirit's Journey* ∞

knowledge in a way that is beneficial for mankind here now, here in the future, and that has already been.

As you walk in this presence know that you are affecting three dimensions in any moment. Your life facets do come forward, around, and through the dimensions that we speak of. It is that which you may refer to as history and future at this space.

We are of the knowledge that there is much polluted area. When we speak of this pollution we are referring to mankind who has been in process of being blocked from their enlightened state. This enlightened state you may refer to as the light is that of release and rapture. True rapture comes from the division, the release of toxic mast cells[1] that are generalized not only in the individual but also in their ancestral root[2].

We are encouraged that you are now processing and aligning to this truth. Release is imperative for this pollution to dissipate.

Individual Messages

Dale: What messages you have for Darlene?

Laura Lyn: You have such unique quality with children and with art. We are hopeful that you will bring forward the natural gifts that you have to help the children grow and move forward in their lives.

Tap into the children that have natural spiritual abilities and you will be helping them learn techniques to help us in the future; to help us clear pollution that was spoken of briefly.

Remember your gifts. They are that which flow through the same energies that flow through Jophiel. Bring forward energy through Archangel Jophiel. You work with the Seraphim so know and understand the angelic energies are flowing through you.

We are understanding that there is a connection from the past. The group that is here now has been together before. This group worked together in tandem to help bring many to a place spiritual alignment through realizing freedom.

What you are working with now is freedom of expression. Your creativity will help the children rise. We encourage you to help the children find their sense of self through the spiritual world.

Tap into the psychic abilities in this natural sense in these children. Please teach the children and you will be aligning your light with a righteous path that is your destiny.

The Dead, the Undead and the Unborn

Dale: What messages do you have for me, Dale?

Laura Lyn: Dale We are very aware of your presence and acknowledge that you have moved so far. We are so eager to see the growth continue. We celebrate in your growth and in your realizing your potentials.

Now please continue to visualize and bring forward your knowledge of technology. You will help continue a path that will bring forward much anticipated growth in what we referred to as spirit soul revival[3].

∞ *The Spirit's Journey* ∞

For this is the way of the world at this point for communication. Allow that energy source to be a source to help the dead, the undead, and the unborn.

Dale: Thank You. Do you have a message for Laura?

Laura Lyn: With Laura we will continue to work through her to help bring universal messages to help people align with their strengths and their gifts.

Laura's purpose is to help people find their gifts and to help bring forward those gifts in a way that will help people find their light. We will help her to find opportunities to help people one at a time through this process.

We are hopeful to see the groups become larger and stronger so that her message can move forward in a more rapid succession. We will continue to help find opportunities and places that she can teach and bring forward that knowledge that will help us arise and bring our message to the world.

Please allow this truth to move forward by allowing the energy through technology, books, and media to be open and we will flow our words forward.

Challenges = Opportunity to Prevail

Dale: Would anyone like to ask a question?

Guest: We each have a difficult child (*from previous marriages*). Do you have any suggestions that would help us to help them find their way?

Our suggestion is that you are the parents and you will continue to work with them closely. The children do have certain difficulties that will prevent them from maturing in a rapid level; however, they will both be adults that you can be proud of with your close supervision.

They will find it necessary to be under your help and resources for quite some time. Understand that this is a gift. Understand that it is part of your journey and your challenge even; however, when you bring forward this in a way of anticipating their growth, you will walk away understanding and seeing the truth that every individual has an opportunity to prevail and move beyond their living potential. What are representing here is that you understand and bring forward your heart as we love you unconditionally; you love your children unconditionally.

Guest: Thank you.

Prosperity Generosity

Dale: Is there anything else that you would like to say to us?

Laura Lyn: We anticipate the growth that will be taking place here, and we understand that there are resources necessary for this growth. We will help you with aligning with prosperity for this prosperity will be for the greater good.

We are asking you to align with the individual community to bring forward a certain percentage to help the community and always bringing forward a percentage to the individual to be very generous and open and we will promise that the flow will come through to bless all.

There will be plenty of opportunities within this group. As long as you stay in that space that Laura refers to as non-

∞ The Spirit's Journey ∞

ego[4] or of the heart you will be in a place of truth and that will align with a measurable perspective for prosperity. We will continue to help bring this potential and expedite the process.

Dale: This session has given us a lot to think about and we thank you all for the messages that you have given us.

Laura Lyn: Thank You.

---

[1] Mast cells – A granular cell found in body tissue, especially connective tissue that activates inflammation by releasing a variety of chemical substances including histamine, tumor necrosis factor, and interleukins. Mast cells have membrane receptors that bind to bacteria, triggering the release of inflammatory mediators from the mast cell's cytoplasmic granules. Mast cells also play an important role in allergic reactions. Other receptors on their membranes bind to specific antibodies that combined with certain antigens, initiate granular release of chemical mediators that cause allergic signs and symptoms.

[2] Ancestral Root – Ancestors from which a person or family is descended.

[3] Soul Revival – another term for Spirit Rescue. This is the first time we heard Spirit Rescue described in this way.

[4] Of the Heart – Truly being more than a representation. Being within who, and what you are.

∞ Realm to Realm ∞

11-9-2010

Spotted Owl, Haley, Carmen
∞

This is another private session. Laura and I are seeking information that will help understand what it's like to be in spirit realm. This is the first session that had a reference to the March 11, 2011 tsunami in Japan.

Spirit Realm, Spirit Self

Dale: We're interested in gathering information about your plane of existence. How does it feel to be where you are?

Laura Lyn: Our existence is as yours. We are free to move upon the earth plane, freely along the grass and with the trees. The difference would be the structure. While we have memories of our structure as they were, we can simply exist upon or within. Meaning that the earth plane or heaven sphere if you will, is as it was in the beginning: unadulterated by human existence.

While we see and feel the structures, we are very aware that we can simply walk through, knowing that it is simply an illusion. Therefore, we are free to move forward, through and around. This helps us to align with the simple truth that existence is within and without substance.

Our truth is, we exist and we are whole and complete within this spirit realm, spirit self. We are spirit through connection to the universal force and place that is the high

∞ *The Spirit's Journey* ∞

reaching sphere which one would call God, but we know as the whole existence of one.

Dale: Are you considered enlightened beings or light workers on our terms? How can we relay where you are as an existence?

Laura Lyn: The human form of today has coined the term light worker. We simply exist in a state of our own enlightenment as individual spirits. We all have our gifts and our awareness that we see through and work through.

We do not anticipate or think of these gifts as functions of a job like state. We simply move forward to learn and to accept in our teachings. Our learned existence helps us become higher frequencies of light. When we refer to light we are referring to purity, pure essences.

We are looking for our being, our spirit being to be whole and complete; releasing any bondage that was presented in the Earth Realm on our physical existence.

Dale: Thank you. How can we relay to people that it is possible to communicate, and how can we relay a means for them to learn to communicate with other planes of existence?

Laura Lyn: As we were referring to, on our realm or our sphere we all learn in our unique manner how to elevate our spirit and purify that Inner light; thereto, people here on the earth realm in the physical state all as individuals will learn in their own way if they expect or have the need to move forward with that communication.

We anticipate that the shackled will be broken free. We anticipate that the future will hold upon itself a time when we can all communicate freely. Crossing these boundaries of restriction that were manmade will take place after the rivers flood and the banks are like a lake. The new flood, the flood that will transform Japan and the countries will sink.

While this happens, there will be many spirits that abound this earth, and the existence of all that spirit supplies and brings forward will be an ocean of currents that need to communicate. At this time the function of communication will take place in an unprecedented amount of time and space. Are you understanding us?

Helping Spirits – Selfless Help

Dale: Yes. We would like to put forth ideas that will help. What is the best way to show people how to communicate?

Laura Lyn: We are concerned with the direction you are taking. For it is the individual expression of the soul to find the way. The individual that has a certain gift or cause to work with the beings, the soul beings, are called into action and can communicate readily.

Those laymen who have just an eager interest to see a ghost or see a spiritual figure, unfortunately, can inhibit the growth of a spiritual being for they place doubt into the spiritual being.

We search for those who are enlightened on your sphere to communicate with us. For you are elevating. For those who are here for mere entertainment, you are hurting us. We are hopeful that the light can shine. We are looking for those who are searching for answers and direction on a spiritual meaning of existence.

We are at a place of hopefulness and even helplessness at the same regard because there are many dying; there are many dying who have lost their way. They are sinking into a deeper abyss within their own making.

Those lost souls who have not gained the insight to release the fear, and the possession of, their making of regret, and the horror of chaos. They are sinking into a deeper abyss of shame, and guilt, sadness. These are the ones we search for you to rescue and are seeking you to help and to honor.

Communicate freely; open yourself to a belief that you can become friends with those that you cannot see. Understand that we hear you; we see you, feel you and know you. As we communicate with you, you will freely see us, know us. It might be in your mind's eye, know we are real.

We are here seeking and searching for answers for our lost ones. We are frightened as they go deeper in that abyss state they will be absorbed into the darkness. Some may call this darkness hell. This darkness, this abyss state is an eternal state until one is ready realize the light within.

We are searching for those that are sinking into the abyss to be aligned with light and truth so they can live, so they can feel, and so they can be full of joy in their cellular essences. When we refer of cellular essence we speak of spiritual awakening within the spiritual matter of truth and light.

Dale: Thank you. Now I wonder, is it our place to help those? Are we actually helping when we do spirit rescue or soul rejuvenation? Are we helping to make a difference?

Laura Lyn: We are hearing you and we can assure you that if the spirit being is entertaining the thought force and listening to you, that they are aligning to truth. Our worry is those who are evoking or not truly believing as they communicate; they are witnessing a spirit wither. It is of the utmost importance that the energy raises and aligns to total belief and that is where the help is.

Dale: I've been attempting to speak to spirits that are around me. Are they hearing me? Am I having the correct intension when I am speaking to them?

Laura Lyn: Yes, communicate and see in your mind's eye what you are gathering.

∞ Realm to Realm ∞

11-15-2010

Spirit Owl, Great Thunder, Great Eagle
∞

We had watched news reports about large amounts of animals dying in different places around the world. We conducted this session to find out what was causing this. We had friends and some of Laura's students join us.

Healing the Earth

Dale: Who is with us this evening?

Laura Lyn: Spirit Owl[1] and Great Thunder[2].

Dale: Thank you for coming forward. We would like to ask some questions about the birds and fish that have been dying. Is there anything you can tell us about that?

Laura Lyn: We have warned and brought forward messages. We have brought forward the great disparity of what is coming forward in this earth. Mother Earth is crying out. She is crying and begging for a solution.

Man is making mistakes and dismal damage to this Earth. She has been crying for resolution, for change, for direction. We are begging you; we are bringing forward messages now through the universe through the space of anguish. We are asking that there will be a solution made to help to save this earth.

The creatures are begging for a solution. There will be a time and a space that the animals will revolt against humans and it is already certainly happening. The creatures are angry. They have been manipulated. They have been exploited. They have been utilized in an incorrect format. This damage is made by greed. It is appalling what has taken place on this earth.

We are disappointed. The damage of the earth is unstoppable at this moment. According to places and people who are in charge of the highest ranks, unfortunately, they do not see what is happening and what they are doing. They do not understand that the earth only has two to three hundred years left under the circumstances that are being presented today.

You are seeing fish and birds die quickly in masses and the governments will say that there are thousands of birds and fish left.

What they do not see is the food chain is being affected right now. There will be many more. Eventually, the birds and the fish will become the deer, goats, cows and the other animals that will eventually take up the whole food chain. Where will the human species find their substance? It is appalling and maddening what is happening to the earth. Again we are disappointed.

We ask, we shout, we beg, and we cry and yet we are not heard. We are ashamed. We are ashamed because we are also of this species that we speak of.

Our present spirit was once human and now here we are seeing the ruins take place by the hand of man. We cry out: please bring forward the message that the energy of destruction must stop.

Guest: Is there anything else that we can do to provide healing to the earth?

Laura Lyn: My child, what we have brought forward is truth. We do understand and appreciate the power of healing. We seek for you to bring forward that message that the healing must take place. We ask that groups will bring forward this consciousness, this healing presence.

We are begging and screaming and shouting for that consciousness to come forward. We search to find these people that will come together to bring the truth. Communities must be built on these truths. The truth is that the world wastes; people waste so much.

The paper cup, the paper plate, the plastic spoon, the waste, the waste that is happening from human species, is filling up the land, the earth. This garbage that is filling the earth is making a toxic destructive hole that is bringing chemicals around the earth and this is killing the minerals within the earth.

There will be no life on earth if this does not stop. Please bring this message forward. Allow that message to be to waste not; be at the space of keeping clean, simple lives that are pure. Live in communities that will help one another.

Guest: If nothing is done, how will the earth last?

Laura Lyn: If nothing is done this earth will not last. Not the way that you are presently seeing it. There is help from other dimensions coming forward. We hope that the help is expedient enough. This earth is very special. She is a special mother. We cry at the thought of her disappearing and drowning.

∞ *The Spirit's Journey* ∞

Guest: Are there any other messages that you can bring forward that we need to know at this time?

Laura Lyn: We beg you to use the winds. We beg you to use the waters. We beg you to use all natural resources possible to bring the energy that is so necessary in today's day. We understand the new way, the new understanding. Without the energy your civilization would cripple.

We are begging for you to find natural ways to sustain this new way of living, this new way of life. We do understand and we are in the process of trying to stop the damage; however, it is the human beings that must make the change possible.

Our predictions can change. There is always choice. We do hope. We do bring forward the blessing. However, we are hearing and seeing that the earth as you know it will die within 300 years if great changes are not now made.

Dale: Many of us feel helpless to be able to make these changes. For many it seems like it is out of our control. What could you tell us about that? How can we as individuals change things?

Laura Lyn: A movement is made so simply by making and bringing forward the vision. You are mirroring a movement by simply being and doing. You have made a movement this summer as you picked up trash from the parks.[3] This was another idea from another dear child. This brought forward a movement of many who are now picking up trash from the forests and streams.

However, the pollution that is here is unnecessary. Teach the ways of the elders to waste none. Start here at home and bring forward your own means of cleansing and allowing the waste to not fill so fast. Look at the ways you can change and teach that. Bring it forward just as you have before.

We are angry. We show our anger at this moment. We are very disappointed. Hear our anger and use that energy; feel it within your own self. The energy that you know is right. That change must take place. Bring forward that energy and make a difference. You have a movement it has started. You have the opportunity to make great change. Gandhi has said be the change. You know that message, you have it within you.

Dale: Thank you. Is there anything else you would like to tell us this evening before I wake Laura up?

Laura Lyn: (*said with anger*) don't be shy. Don't be embarrassed. If you alienate yourself from others they weren't ready to hear the message anyhow. Don't feel forceful when you're bringing forward this message. If people feel uncomfortable it's only because they know deep within that they are also guilty. There is no one, very, very seldom are there people who are not guilty in this. This has become a chaotic mess, a chaotic whirlwind tornado.

There is poison spewed all over this earth. There are people that are head of states, head of powers that are very aware of what is happening. Share this message. Bring it forward. We are crying out to you to make a difference.

Guest: We will do our best, but it seems almost impossible. There is so much pollution.

Laura Lyn: It is sad that Mother Earth will take care of herself and that is true. The shame is that there will be a very miniscule number of creatures upon her to share her spirit. She will be alone and that makes us sad. We are saddened yet we are hopeful.

The Shift – Reincarnation – Love - Soul Groups

Laura Lyn: Great Eagle[4] would like to speak.

Dale: Hello Great Eagle.

Laura Lyn: (*softer tone*) We would like to bring forward a vision. While there are many dying, we ask you to understand that there are three worlds at any time that are being affected. Understand when masses of birds, or fish or people die that there are connections from the past. You may refer to this as soul groups, soul reunions.

There are natural patterns that take place that do bring forth a time, when it is appropriate, where many souls will die in a collection. This is cyclic and natural. This is a rhythm that takes place in life. You have heard the message that there is a shift, a great shift, taking place presently. There have been many prophets that have brought forward this knowledge.

Just as there is a natural order and cleansing that takes place where there is a multitude of hundreds and thousands of people who are taken from life, sustained life on this earth, from natural causes such as a tsunami. There are also natural rhythms where a soul collection will take place from the fowl, the fish, the feathered ones, the species of the earth.

∞ Realm to Realm ∞

The Hindan understand that people may come forward in different subspecies that are not necessarily human species. The fish may be your grandmother the worm your grandfather. We ask and seek that you protect all species of the earth as if they were your own for they do have the knowledge. The worm crawls on the earth; she understands the heartbeat of the mother.

We ask that you seek refuge with your families and you bring forward communication about the importance of community. Share your messages that you hear through the universe, through Great Spirit, through Spirit Owl. Understand that the messages are coming from a space of love and light. These messages these are the answers that people are seeking.

In bringing forward the messages you are bringing forward healing, inspiration, and empowerment. Allow the great eagle to soar and that is the great message. The message of peace, love, and honor of all; this is the message of oneness. We are all here together.

The species are a collection of the universal consciousness. This power, this beautiful power, came from a loving source and it started by a particle and a sub-particle. It is now in a cyclic place of evolvement.

You will find the peace in this, the harmony in this, and the simplicity. Allow your spirit to soar. Fear not, allow the change to happen within your heart and all will be well. Thank you.

Dale: Thank you.

∞ The Spirit's Journey ∞

[1] Spirit Owl –Universal consciousness

[2] Great Thunder – Native American Enlightened being who is fighting pollution and destruction of Mother Earth.

[3] You have made a movement this summer as you picked up trash from the parks – every effort can make a difference.

[4] Great Eagle - Native American Enlightened being

∞ Realm to Realm ∞

11-16-2010

Great Spirit, Raphael, Edgar Cayce

∞

Helping Spirits – Talking to Spirits

This session brought some excellent insights. The information presented here gave all of us a new perspective on spirit existence. Stephanie was here with us. I asked more questions about how things work from a spirit's perspective.

Dale: How can we help the earth bound spirits? Are they addicted to being in a physical state?

Laura Lyn: Many feel trapped in their own thought patterns and beliefs. The truth is that no being is trapped as there is always choice.

When you speak of addiction to this physical state, what is truth is they are remembering what life was, what life felt like, and they are trying to reenter this life state through human existence. Unfortunately, they never understood that they were mere representations of spirit through the life force, life form, of skeletal system and skin, and that peaceful place is that karmetic place[1]; that heaven sphere[2] is all around.

We are understanding your question and are asking you to bring forward the information to the spirit presence (the human beings that were once upon this earth and walking upon the earth as the "dead") that they have a choice and they can move forward in their state and their being, finding that light within as it was always within. Help them to remember who they are; Spirit presence, the one, as always and always will be.

Earth Bound

Dale: Are earth bound spirits able to hear us more readily than they can hear other spirits that don't have a physical form?

Laura Lyn: The truth is that the spirits that you are communicating with can't see other spiritual beings, because they are unaware that they are dead. They have refused to believe that they are dead. They are walking among us here on earth, walking among men, very unaware that they are not in a present state of life. So they are unaware of the presence of spirit all around them.

Dale: To them it feels as if they are right here still alive walking the earth?

Laura Lyn: That is correct.

Dale: Why is it that some of us can see spirits and others can't?

Laura Lyn: Some people have a natural ability because they are in that spirit presence themselves. They have a spirit presence that is very unique and aligned to that presence. Others, while it can be acquired through patience and practice, can take a lifetime journey to get to that presence.

It is a muscle or a connection inward where you can align to that place to be able to see. But we ask you to feel and know the spirit is around you and through that space and through that place you can see.

See in a different way than thorough your two eyes. You can see them through your inner knowing. The presence, the spirit is beside you, among you, and all around.

Dale: We are attempting to communicate with Spirit. We would very much like to communicate. Is it the daily distractions in life that make that difficult?

Laura Lyn: You are both open vessels. You are both gifted vessels to communicate with spirit. Trust yourself. When you hear the words coming in, trust them. It is the mere understanding that truth will always communicate with you, and you always ask for truth.

The energies that intertwine within you daily are the vessels, the messengers, the peacemakers, the ones that love, the vibration of nirvana, which is here to help you bring forward a message. But remember that this is always in a spirit of helping others and in the space of that truth within the heart.

If you are here honestly to bring forward energy to help others, the energy will always be here to help you. Be in that space and the energy will increase.

You are both, Stephanie and Dale, opening to that space in a beautiful way and it is entwined with love. We are honored to work with both of you.

Stephanie: This is going to take practice and patience.

Dale: And I think it is listening more to ourselves.

Laura Lyn: I think it's both. Because this is a space that you are trusting yourself: Listening, hearing, speaking, knowing, feeling; bringing it together in a face of love. You are always in a place, a presence, with the spirit that we speak of. Those enlightened ones that are with you on your journey will always be there to speak through you as long as your heart is open to hear their words.

Dale: Thank you again. That is very nice to hear. Are there any messages that you would just like us to bring forward? Or anything you would like to tell us?

Laura Lyn: Yes, we have a favor to ask both of you. We are in a space of desperation and we are asking for assistance if you will. We see the world is being polluted. The pollution we speak of is untruth of hatred, greed, and the desire to stop love.

Dale: What can people do to help?

Laura Lyn: People are hearing the message. Even those that do not understand now, will understand at a later point. And those that don't resonate completely have still heard the words, and felt the energy, and may make a decision at a later time.

Dale, you have asked many questions about your journey. You see that their journey is bringing deeper truths and how important this is. At this space and time you are bringing forward knowledge and in this knowledge, it will become well applied through your energy you seek. You seek for deliberate precision, momentum, a pace. You are seeking knowledge.

You are putting it together for others to understand the subtle energies that are all around. Keep moving forward in this direction. You see how important it is for Stephanie and you, and others to work together in this vision.

There is truth in all. Please bring forward this truth and you will be helping people find this peace and place of love. Stephanie and Dale please work together to bring this truth. We are honored that you are both here.

Dale: thank you. We are honored by your messages. I thank you for validating my quest for knowledge. I'm enjoying every minute of it. It has been my daily work to share what I'm learning. I'm making absolutely sure that it's good knowledge.

Stephanie: I have to agree with Dale I feel the same way. My life has changed dramatically and I'm not the same person. I feel different.

Laura Lyn: You are a pure essence of truth. Everybody in this world, everybody in this place, is where they are for a reason on their journey. You are a more perfected ray of hope, truth, and peace. In that vibration you can help others get to that place where you are now. We will help you on this path.

Dale: Thank You.

---

[1] Karmetic place –Each of us has our own karma to work through. We will be where our karma allows. Karma is ultimately within and also without. There are no scorekeepers, no levels.

[2] Heaven Sphere – This term is used to describe the Earth and other states of being.

∞ *The Spirit's Journey* ∞

∞ Realm to Realm ∞

1-19-2011

Haniel, Raphael and Spirit Owl

∞

This session was intended to help gather information about releasing thought habits, past guilt and fears.

Laura Lyn: Enlightened messengers, enlightened beings, those who would like to come forward to help with this process. Where we would like to get some information about release of guilt and turmoil, internal turmoil to not only help him but help others in the process. Spirit, we are saying thank you. We are grateful for your presence. We are asking that any messengers come forward to help us with this process.

Dale: Please let me know when you are ready for questions.

Laura Lyn: We are here.

Dale: Who is with us tonight?

Laura Lyn: Haniel, Raphael and Spirit Owl are present.

We are all Together

Dale: Is there anything you would like to tell us tonight?

Laura Lyn: The process that everyone and everything is connected is pertinent for today's teachings, for it brings back the great truth that all is one and one is all.

We are all together, every one of us: spirit, people that are here on the earth, that are alive, and then those that are here in a different dimension entirely. We are here

∞ The Spirit's Journey ∞

connected through the fibers of the universe, the layers of a great source. (Everything is connected)

Within the fibers of this energy there are cells that bring in a wonderful truth. This truth that we are speaking of is about helping to bring forward healing energies; allowing each other to heal to their greatest capacity.

By aligning to your authentic self, you are being that truth; every day being in the spirit of helping your brothers and sisters. This is where the message flows.

Dale: Many people we know, including me, seem to have something blocking their progress. It seems like it's from the past and it's not on a conscious level. Is there anything you can tell us about that?

Laura Lyn: You have within you all the tools necessary to help you release the traumas from the past. Within your own self, you have a healing capacity by simply believing, being aware, and courageous. Allow yourself to come to a place where you know and understand that you are indeed filled with harmony.

You have within you, within the sphere of your heart, the ability to release the pain so that it is only a simple memory. Allow your heart to soar through the truth of love; love for yourself, for others, and for the beauty in life.

You will capture yourself smiling and being in that full brilliant place of joy. Joy is the essence you are following in. That is the place where this healing will take place. Please remember that you have the tools within you; release, allow the energies to flow forward. Become aware of the Supreme Being around you in every step. Believe in that being and when we refer to the Supreme Being, we are referring all the energy encompassing you. Allow your courageous heart to soar.

Feel the pride, and allow that pride to come forward into your heart to believe in yourself. Pride and ego are separate. Allow that pride to move forward in your heart to allow the heart to heal. Believe in yourself, have courage and faith, and walk in this beautiful path. We respect you; we honor you, and thank you for the question.

Dale: Thank you. Do you have anything else you would like to tell us?

Seekers on this Earth

Jessica: New spiritual doorways have been opening for me lately and I have an idea what they might mean. I didn't know if I am correct in my thinking.

Laura Lyn: We are pleased that pathway is showing itself so clearly to you. We understand that you are starting to understand the shamanic pathway[1] has been your past and becoming your present.

There is more to your doorway that will be opening. You have within you magic. Allow the plants to speak to you. You will be bringing forward your magic that you receive to help bring healing. You will help detoxify and heal.

The devotion that you will be bringing forward will help Mother Earth heal. Trust your vision and trust yourself. This is a time of learning. This is a great time in your life path. Be grateful and wise with this chosen time in your life path. Trust the path. It is opening wide for you.

We are thankful for you have become a seeker. We need seekers on this earth. Your pure energy and essence is a welcomed gift to Mother Earth. Thank you, Jessica.

Dale: I'm wondering about releasing and accepting on an emotional level. It seems like my subconscious wants to pull me back. Do you have any suggestions?

Laura Lyn: You are in a habitual form at a point of self-preservation. With that habit you have brought yourself to a vibration that is difficult to move forward. While we understand that at this moment you may be feeling uncomfortable by hearing these words, we feel it is important to bring them to you as this is the way of healing.

We are understanding that the habitual place that your brain resonates brings back chaos, sadness and fears. The truth is while many from your past were not emotionally equipped to fully love, you are now surrounded by total love. The reality is that rejection is not likely to occur, but the habit, the mere habit of being rejected in the past was very real.

Dale: Thank you. I will do what I can.

Dale: Do you have anything else you would like to share with us?

Prepare Yourself for the Future

Laura Lyn: We understand that there are great disturbances upon the earth at this moment. We are under the influence of what will happen in the near future with a great flood. You are seeing around the world pockets of floods.[2] It is just the beginning.

∞ Realm to Realm ∞

Please prepare yourself for the future, while it is not this part of the world, your attention, insight, and healing will be necessary and we are preparing you that there will be great loss.

Please keep strong and open for there will be a time when spirit is asking for your collective assistance. To bring a rapid healing to those that are saved they will surely need spiritual assistance to help them in their life path. We are asking for a conscious connection on a synergetic level that will be powerful to bring healing to the flooded lands.

Dale: And when you're speaking of preparation are you speaking of our physical needs or are you speaking of spiritual?

Laura Lyn: I am speaking of prayerfully being ready to help those in need.

Dale: Do you have any timeframe on our terms when something like this is going to happen?

Laura Lyn: We are anticipating by the spring a great flood.

Dale: OK. Is this all part of the shift we've been learning of in 2012?

Laura Lyn: It is likely; however, there are natural occurrences that are happening within the earth's sphere. That is, the outer core that will bring forward the moisture. That will bring this flood forward.

Dale: Are you talking about the polar ice caps melting?

Laura Lyn: We are speaking of natural occurrences in the waves that will bring forward condensation in a great space. We are anticipating this will take many nations to a new level, and we fear their energy will not transcend. Therefore; they will need many prayers to help them release and rejuvenate. Your work will be needed to help these precious souls to transcend.

The Earth is Alive

Dale: We'll do our best. We'll discuss this with Laura. I've been talking among friends and most of us have felt that there are too many people, and what is going on with the earth is just a natural cycle.

Laura Lyn: The earth can handle many people. People must learn to handle the earth; handle the earth with love and compassion as you would your mother, your brother, your sister.

The people must learn that the earth is alive, a living vessel that is here to help sustain people.

The people must learn that the Mother, the Earth, has a heartbeat, has a rhythm, and a cycle, just as a human cycle.

When people learn to honor the Mother there will be plenty of space. When there is no longer space on this earth, potentially there could be space on other worlds. However, if this world, this earth, and the inhabitants move forward in this same direction as they are presently, there will be no more people to sustain for they are killing their selves with the toxins that they are dumping into Mother Earth.

Dale: Thank You. That gives us a lot to think about. Do you have anything else Jessica?

∞ *Realm to Realm* ∞

Awakening yourself spiritually

Jessica: Why have I been experiencing different emotional and physical manifestations?

Laura Lyn: This is a natural process of awakening yourself spiritually. You are aligning to vibrations that are quite different than you were subjected to in the past. Be gleeful and happy for this expression that you are receiving, and be comfortable, for this is a time and place that you will be rapidly shifting, vibrationally and internally.

We are quite pleased that you are moving forward so quickly. Be in balance and peace in this space as you have found home. The home we speak of is that place within your heart and your soul, the beauty within.

You are now in the midst of remembering who you are. And in that beauty you can transcend and bring forward the magic that was always within. You can bring it forward to other hearts that are searching for their truth. That is where beauty lies, and beauty is. Walk in beauty dear, and you will be bringing harmony to the land.

Jessica: Thank you.

Dale: Do you have anything else to say before I wake Laura up?

Laura Lyn: We are finished. Thank you.

Dale: And we thank you. I would like to ask that you help Laura wake up and come back to us. Once again I really thank you.

∞ *The Spirit's Journey* ∞

[1] Shamanic Pathway - A member of certain tribal societies who acts as a medium between the visible world and an invisible spirit world and who practices magic or sorcery for purposes of healing, divination, and control over natural events.

[2] Floods – at this time there were floods in Australia, China, and California.

∞ Realm to Realm ∞

2-15-2011

Great Spirit, Edgar Cayce
∞

Laura Lyn: We are asking to protect all of us during this process. We are asking for enlightened beings and guides to come through to allow information to be very clear and concise. We are asking for only the greatest good, the greatest light, and the greatest love during this process so that while I go into this sleeping trance the information can come forward for universal knowledge and truth to share, to bring out to help people, to align to deeper meaning of God Consciousness. I'm asking to go into that place of drifting so that the messages can be very clear and concise. I'm feeling myself drifting now thank you. I can feel them here.

Dale: Is Laura ready to speak?

Laura Lyn: She is ready.

Dale: Who's with us today?

Laura Lyn: We have Great Spirit, Edgar Cayce, Spirit Owl, Raphael

Love - The Prosperity of the Future

Dale: Is there anything you would like to say to us today?

Laura Lyn: We are very pleased with this reunion, a new beginning, a new birth, a new life. As this transition begins, understand that there is energy that is at this moment of truth that is guided and blessed in this union[1].

∞ The Spirit's Journey ∞

We are here, and will be here, to celebrate this new truth, new light, and as the challenges present themself we will be here to bring order, balance, and quick action. The truth is, that the reunion is not only of Dale and Laura but moves much deeper.

There are people gathering together and amongst your present state that are very critical for growth on a planetary basis and there will be changes happening rapidly that will enable a new balance of happiness and joy, peace, and serenity.

The truth is, that monetary frequencies will not carry the importance as it once did. Love will far exceed the value, and love will be the prosperity of the future. This is what your new friends and family devotion were pragmatically and functionally chosen for. You have all been chosen to bring forward a new way, a new light, and a new word to this land.

We are pleased that you are hearing these words. Love, as we speak of it, goes much deeper than romantic or friendship type of love that the human self often feels. We are talking about an everlasting flow of consciousness, of light, a frequency of light that enables pure healing essence in every vessel. This is the vibrational change that is taking place.

Your soul group that is here present will be largely enabling this process. We thank you.

Dale: Thank you.

Monica: **I have a question for Edgar Cayce if I may. After reading some of your material I was wondering if**

part of the reason we currently use only 10 percent of our brain is because we have lost a lot of the gifts and innate abilities we were originally given when we came here. If that is correct is there a way to learn those things and teach younger generations to use those gifts and get back what we have lost?

You are correct, with exception. While people are born with a plethora of gifts, we cannot state that everyone is gifted in the same precise amount. There is no need for everyone to be born with the same quality or quantity of gifts, because according to their plan of life some would never be utilized.

So therefore, there are a plethora of gifts brought forward per person, per unit, per cell if you will, and that gift or that frequency is aligned, perfected to the highest potential at birth.

You can re-invite or re-align with a precise frequency by understanding that you are true energy, true consciousness of God within and through every frequency of your body.

As you tap into that knowledge, simply understanding that it is within you; you are then sourcing that re-frequenced gift, and the alignment will take place.

Ask and you shall receive. Believe and it is given. It is that simple.

What happens is that the energies get redirected so quickly because of doubt, fear, misunderstanding. Align with truth and insight that you have the potential within you to tap into that consciousness that we refer to as God, the pure power of love. Knowing that all will be realigned to that perfected order. Thank you, dear child.

Monica: Thank you.

Detached Spirit – Physical Self

Jessica: There have been several incidents where my mom and dad have seen me in my house when I'm not there. We wanted to know if this is a doppelganger[2] and perhaps why it happens.

Laura Lyn: OK, we understand that there is a projection of your soul-source or your soul-self in a physical body. Is the question what this represents or means? Please clarify.

Monica: I think what she's asking is that her parents have seen her form without her physically being there how can that occur and what would cause that?

Laura Lyn: Thank you for the precision. We are understanding the question. We will refer to this as a spirit-self. Sometimes our spirit-self detaches. Many may refer to that as the Higher Self.[3]

When there is change or transition often times there is disconnectedness from the physical body form. The spirit-self, the soul-self and the physical body are not completely united in those moments.

Always ask that your higher self or your inner spirit[4] is closely woven so there are no disturbances. Disconnectedness is an unfortunate circumstance that can take place during these times of great evolution.

Our physical self here on earth has a static form where the frequency would like to stay within the status quo and the spirit self would like to move forward and enjoy the new truth, the new light.

Amongst that vulnerability darkened energies can come forward and let's say "seize the moment" and trap the physical self into the old ways.

Please always be conscious of this and ask your higher self to stay with your physical self at all times. Keeping yourself secure and shielded will help you move forward in that higher vibration.

Are we clear in this understanding?

Jessica: Yes, thank you.

Laura Lyn: Thank you

Round out our Whole Being

Dale: Can you tell us something about our history, past lives?

Laura Lyn: We understand your questions and would like to proceed by explaining some history. Dale, as you know you have been with Laura many life streams in the past. And you understand and remember correct that you have been part of her life stream in the male and female embodiment, the masculine and the feminine.

Laura Lyn: We have a question for you that is very important and we mean no disrespect.

Dale: Ok.

Laura Lyn: In your searching at this present moment, are you happy?

Dale: Yes, I am happy.

∞ *The Spirit's Journey* ∞

Laura Lyn: Are you understanding in your past there was much pain and confusion?

Dale: I'm feeling it, I guess the specifics aren't important is that what you are telling me?

Laura Lyn: No, before we share your past with you, we want you to understand every life time span had direction and reason. This may sound startling and we want to prepare you. Do you understand?

Dale: Yes.

A significant part of your loss and confusion has been caused by history. You were murdered by Laura. It was actually not a murder but a condemned rightful act (*Capital punishment*).

He (Laura) was rightfully given the act to take this man's life for this man had taken another. And while he felt condemned and was maddened temporarily through that process, he was directed to do this.

This is a complex situation. You are faced with fear because of a life lost. Understand this took place for Karmic reaction[5] for a previous casualty. We understand this is now consciously cleared from your pathway.

Dale: So just to make this clear. Throughout our lifetimes, we experience and we express different circumstances and situations to round out our whole being.

Laura Lyn: Yes, to round out your whole existence.

Dale: So our goal while in the physical realm is to experience, express, and develop a well-rounded existence?

Laura Lyn: That is precise truth.

Dale: And that is what we are doing right now?

Laura Lyn: That is truth, however there is more, so much more. It is imperative for the human existence to be here on this world so the information is interpreted through what we would refer to as God or the source of power.

We are now at a time where this frequency is raising. In that vibration, the shields are needed to combat the darkened energies for they will inevitably conquer the world if love does not sustain. So in that frequency of love and honor is the truth of why existence is here. Existence is here for love and honor of self through the expression of God, and existence of joy, joy of life.

We are here to free the land so that the world can be in a new place where wars and murder is not necessary. For there will be a time near that other worlds can be taken up through technology, and the population can grow, and the spirits can be released. The three worlds, the dead, the undead and the unborn can rebalance. So this is a critical time to teach love and honor. Thank you Dale.

---

[1] *This is three days before we got married. The wedding began as a surprise birthday party that somehow turned into a wedding with three days to prepare.*

∞ The Spirit's Journey ∞

[2] Doppelganger – A mirror image of oneself, a double, also described as alter ego

[3] Spirit self, Higher self – The term higher self, spirit self are two of many ways to describe our internal being.

[4] Inner spirit – Another term to describe the higher self

[5] Karmic reaction – Throughout our numerous lives, we experience all possible situations in order to round out our existence. Someone you see now who is facing extreme struggles in this life may have been very happy and successful in a previous life. This seems to negate judgment. All has purpose.

∞ Realm to Realm ∞

3-20-2011

Spirit Owl, Raphael and Edgar Cayce
∞

Dale: Who's with us this evening?

Laura Lyn: We have Spirit Owl, Raphael and Edgar Cayce.

Dale: What would you like to tell us this evening?

Cleansing Mother Earth

Laura Lyn: There is a presence of turmoil on Mother Earth. This is divine for in that chaotic space many lessons and deeds are being followed through.

The resolution that is forming at this precise moment is that of honor. We are bringing forth energy into this great planet, into this great space and earth and in that space transcendence is surely following.

The Dead, the Undead and the Unborn

A cleansing is happening to Mother Earth. Understand this is a sacred time; for the cleansing is also an opening. You will see many more tears as the rivers fill, the seas will follow and great winds will travel.

While we understand that the tears will drop, with each tear that falls on Mother Earth, a sacred cleansing is happening. The heavens will open and the dead, the undead, and the unborn, will find their right place unto this earth and into the realms of the Great Mother.

This a holy time. While you see the fighting upon the lands the religious rights of the ancestors are being

∞ *The Spirit's Journey* ∞

reclaimed and there will be a place of balance and freedom in your future for these countries.

At this moment the chains are being broken, and in the wars the rights of man and woman are being realized. The war that is at this precise moment in Libya is that of a village. A deep ancestral root from the past is being cleansed.

It is right to let the fight flow and to see the freedom reign. This will happen in your lifetime and you will be glad. And as the freedoms come forward and the unity begins and in that you will find harmony and peace. Thank you for being here and hearing our words. We are honored to speak.

A Plethora of Spirit

Dale: Who was just speaking?

Laura Lyn: Spirit Owl is my name. However, I am a plethora of spirit. I am divine word that comes from many tongues, lands, and realms. I am what you would refer to as universal energy. In this space I am all, and all is one connected. We bring forward messages from many entities and beings, from many spaces and times. And in this moment you are speaking to Edgar Cayce, Spirit Owl and Raphael.

Dale: Thank you.

Simply a Thought Away - Japan Tsunami

Dale: Do you have more that you would like to tell us?

Laura Lyn: We are saddened by all the knowledge of the floods that were forewarned. The energy that we are speaking of, in our saddened space is the regrets and fears from those who have passed. We are striving to help these souls but understand that you may reach them before we may, for they may hear your presence before ours.

At this time, they are more frequenced to hear the living than that of spirit. And while your languages are quite different, they will still hear you and understand your love. We invite you to have a soul meeting with those that have passed and are still lost.

We are grateful and hopeful that you will move forward and speak to these men, women, and children who are lost and in fear. Even though the distance may be far and wide here on earth, the spirit world is quite different and simply a thought away.

You may move through the veil and touch into the energy. Just your thought and intent will help them toward that great light, that great frequency and vibration of truth. We hope you hear our words and help these beautiful souls find unity and peace.

Dale: Can we do this in groups and individually?

Laura Lyn: It's something that you can do internally through meditation, externally in groups in your spirit circles, or you may teach others. It is correct how you work to help rejuvenate the soul. Trust yourself and move forward with teaching others.

∞ *The Spirit's Journey* ∞

Spirit Realm and Human Realm are Together

Jan: Spirit Owl, I wanted to know if you have any messages for Laura, Dale or I as individuals.

Laura Lyn: We bring forward these messages. Dale we are hopeful that you continue to follow the path and understand that you have a sacred path here; a rich path where you are learning and seeking the knowledge, the holy knowledge, which was passed on from Rudolph Steiner.

What you are hearing is correct for the book will be compiled messages that relay the spirit and human realms are one together. The physical, spiritual, and emotional are all one.

This will help bring a connection that many are seeking in this confusing time. We thank you for hearing our words and this important work. The world they need your word. We are grateful Dale.

Dale: Thank you, I am grateful for everything that I'm hearing.

Laura Lyn: We are grateful for this time to speak and we seek now to rest. Thank you.

∞ Realm to Realm ∞

3-30-2011

Edgar Cayce, White Dove and Chief White Feather

∞

Spirit Perspective – Many Spirits

Dale: Are you ready to speak with us?

Laura Lyn: I'm drifting right now. I'm still here. But I want to share with you what I'm involved in. There are hundreds of spirits present. It's all these faces looking at me, anticipating a message. But they are not looking at me they are looking through my eyes but...Edgar Cayce is here present and it's his eyes they are looking at. It's very interesting. And there are two others here present...

Dale: Do you have their names?

Laura Lyn: One I have never seen before or witnessed. We are here present.

Dale: Who is with us this evening?

Laura Lyn: Edgar Cayce, White Dove[1], and Chief White Feather.

Dale: What would you like to tell us tonight?

The Heart Dwells in Light – The Shift

Laura Lyn: There are many messages, one voice. We are here in preparation for a great change, a great challenge. We are in the midst of allowing the energies to pour forward a new direction that will haunt some and bring

∞ *The Spirit's Journey* ∞

relief to others. You may know this as the awakening or the shift.

This is a space of tranquility for some and a daunting chaotic force for others. Where you are merely depends on the trust you have in your heart, for the truth is within the span of your heart space. The truth is within you.

I am **White Dove** and I am here to bring forward peace. The peace that you understand within your sphere radiates outwards when you deliver that heart forward. Trust in your own healing capacity. There is a great mission when you realize your potential.

As the dove signifies peace, understand the wings can fly higher and the potential is indeed great. Be in that space of peace, for this is the movement of freedom, a direction for change, a place for delivered beauty.

I have been known as a princess, I have been known as a warrior and as a king. I come from a space of wisdom, a village that was raptured and a kingdom that was won. I have many experiences where a village pulled together a great place of prosperity and in that space the village truly became one. Trust that place and all will be good.

I am an old wise woman. Hear my words. The feminine pathway[2] is where prosperity will follow. The prosperity I speak of is that prosperous heart bringing a powerful love cord, remembering the children, the joy of the child. Bring yourself back to that eager eye.

In that eager eye you will see a new direction. You are truly one. There is no separate energy when it comes to the human race. Brothers and sisters: band together to bring the truth to the land that the heart dwells in light.

Spirit Rescue

Dale: Thank you for the beautiful message White Dove.

Laura Lyn: Thank you for hearing my message dear ones.

Dale: Can you tell us about our spirit rescue we did this evening[3]?

Laura Lyn: There were many angels and guided ones together with deep gratitude for the love that was brought forward. Together this beautiful energy allowed the fear to dissipate.

Feel the warmth in the room, in the space now. Know that you dwell in a space that has been enlightened, just as the souls found their enlightenment. Hundreds upon hundreds of souls are finding their space in groups such as this across the world. What was brought forward is helping the souls free and we are very grateful for this.

Trust what you are seeing and hearing. Trust the certain knowing that is moving forward through your sacral. Trust the knowledge you receive is of truth. Trust what you see and allow the words to move forward. The uttered words upon the tongue are righteous words that are received in the utmost respect and honor. Continue the work. It is good. Thank you.

∞ The Spirit's Journey ∞

Release and Grief

Dale: We have our friend Sheryl here today. What would you like to tell her?

Laura Lyn: Sheryl, thank you for being here. We are truly blessed that your presence is here. Your heart is very pure and loving. All you know is love. The pain that came upon you when your husband passed was tremendous. We witnessed and sat with you during the time of release and grief.

We have always been present with you and your children and are grateful that you found your way here with your friends and family. The truth is dear one that you have a unique and loving gift to offer. There is a deep purpose to allow your heart to shine continually for you are bringing healing to a space that is so necessary.

Finding this light within and acknowledging this light will help you to become your authentic self. Your healing presence through your heart is powerful and with that energy, you will help transcend souls. Continue the work in this presence of light for it is good. Light strength comes forward through your heart in this presence.

Understand that you have links from the past with some who are here with you. Understand that this is a soul pathway that was brought forward[4]. We honor you and love you dear one and we thank you for your presence.

Past Life Situation

Monica: Edgar I have several questions. One of which is Laura's neck. Could you tell me what is going on, and if there is something that can help her?

Laura Lyn: The neck has many facets with the damage that has brought forward pain. C2 is compressed from many whiplashes that were sustained in the past. A problem lies within a past life a past situation when Laura was hung. While she has released a great deal of this entity from the past, and she released a great deal through the cellular memory, there still remains a sustained amount of energy that when released will help decompress C2.

The problem lies within this past lifespan for the hanging was not immediate and there was sustained pain. Helping release that energy will dissipate the radiating discomfort that is moving through the bodily system. With C2 compression understand that the heart quadrant is being complicated and helping with decompression would be very powerful.

Past Lives Sheryl

Laura Lyn: This is for Sheryl. Sheryl, this is Chief White Feather[5]. I am proud and honored to be your friend you have brought forward mighty courage for your family. I have witnessed you bring forward the energy to help sustain your family in a powerful way, a mighty way.

You are a blessed mother to your children and they ought to be proud of their mother. You are a blessed elder and teacher to your children and you teach peace. I want to honor you for you are indeed the blood of the clan. You have endured the warrior. You have fought hard and delivered peace.

You have strength, courage and a will that has sustained. You still have the eager eyes of the child. The eagle honors you and will be your friend. Watch for the sign from the eagle and there you will soar. Your presence is bright. Understand that this presence of love is true. We are here to thank you dear one.

You are at Peace

Laura Lyn: Dale, we have a message from your grandfather. He wants you to know that he knew the pain that you had in your life. He was always aware. He is glad of where you are and the peace that you have found.

He loves you dearly as your grandmother does. You are in a new space now and he begs you to release the past. He is moving forward now, knowing that you are at peace. He will be bringing help to others for this is his mission, his ministry.

He is hopeful that you will be able to release the past, to forgive, and to move forward in the knowledge that everybody did the best that they could do with the knowledge that they had. You were never alone and were always protected. Release the loneliness and the fear; it is time.

The kindness that is shown upon you by your wife and friends is real. Hold onto that and realize that you are worthy of this love. Hear the truth. There is no need to harbor any of the old memories and keep them alive. Allow them to be memories such as a movie; release and restore.

Allow the guidance of the love that is in your presence to be your teacher. You are a very wise man. You have strength and courage. You sustained much pain and

∞ Realm to Realm ∞

loneliness. Now is the crossroad to release that loneliness and understand that love surrounds you.

There is never a reason to feel alone, to have judgment, fear, or any regret. We hope that you will hold this message and carry it in your heart. Thank you.

---

[1] White Dove – Native American Spirit Guide.
[2] Feminine Pathway – The path of living in compassion also considered to be a path of balance.
[3] Spirit Circle - *We had just finished a spirit circle with friends who are students and graduates from Laura's psychic development classes. We witnessed many spirit rescues during the circle. It seemed that the room was completely filled with spirits.*

[4] Soul pathway – Many friends and family are within our soul family or soul group. This is referring to a calling for reunion.
[5] Chief White Feather - Native American Spirit Guide.

∞ *The Spirit's Journey* ∞

∞ Realm to Realm ∞
4-4-2011
Great Spirit, Rudolf Steiner, Edgar Cayce
∞

Monica: Should we begin with questions or is there a message we should receive first?

Unity Holds Truth for All

Laura Lyn: Our presence has been here for the following reason. We are here to bring messages of hope to all brothers and sisters. Allow joy of life to be the ultimate destiny. Learning the knowledge of helping one another, this is true light.

We are seeing unity develop across the world as the tragedy (of Japan) has come forward. Life can only sustain where love and unity holds truth for all. Thank you.

Overcoming Stress

Monica: Who's with us tonight?

Laura Lyn: We have Spirit Owl, we have Great Spirit and we have Edgar Cayce.

Monica: I'd like to direct my questions at Edgar Cayce if that is ok?

Laura Lyn: Please my dear.

Monica: Edgar I am having a real struggle with school. I feel overwhelmed by my stress level. And I have a real fear that I'm not going to make it through this program. I need to know how to best study, how to center myself

∞ *The Spirit's Journey* ∞

and how to get past any blocks I have. I feel that I know this deep down already, but it's just so much so fast.

Laura Lyn: We have been with you and understand that your current life situation has overwhelming stress and difficulties. We are asking you to please rest more. Your energy level is being depleted at a rapid state.

The water in your system is depleting. Please oxygenate your water. I am asking you to look at Gingko Biloba tincture 3 drops in the morning in 8 fluid oz. of water.

Do not forget my dear that the universe flows through your fingertips. The energy at the crown chakra[1] and the third eye can be brought forward at any moment by merely touching your fingertips to the crest of your head and to the center of your forehead. Allow those energies to flow inward and the studies will be attained.

Allow yourself in the evening to prepare with a salt bath. The sea salts will release the toxicities. This will help you exponentially.

During the afternoon hour's prayer is essential. Allow yourself 5 minutes of prayer in the afternoon, prayer for your family, children, friends, and yourself to be guided by God's love. God is here present always within you, within your spirit.

You have the answers and the information is flowing. Allow Metatron[2] to be part of your process for he holds those great keys of knowledge within the Akashic records.

Light a candle three days before your exam and invite Metatron's energy to flow. This will invoke his great spirit energy. His essence will be a part of you. You will pass, and you will move forward. You will heal many people in the future. Thank you.

Life Choices - Purpose

Monica: Thank you. Can I ask one more question?

Laura Lyn: Yes please.

Monica: What did I come into the world choosing to do this time because I feel I've messed everything up?

Laura Lyn: My dear you made no mistakes in this world. You fell in love with a man seeing his light and potential and in that there is no harm.

He chose a different way and we are saddened. He decided on a direction that will be difficult and harsh. His destiny is to work through the shadow self because this is his decision.

Pray for him but let him go my dear for in your truth and path, you have made a decision to help bring light and there will be another brought to you in the future.

You will not be alone we promise that. Your children are your destiny now as they always were. You have an opportunity to help bring these beautiful children into a world that is filled with their light.

Trust your pathway my dear. We love you and will always work with you.

Prayer Groups

Monica: We were talking this evening about how to build up a foundation of prayer. Do you have a suggestion for that?

Laura Lyn: We invite this concept; weekly prayer and healing sessions for devotion and reflection to bring prosperous energy and love.

Monica: Thank you. We have all been feeling a little bit uneasy in our energy. Is there a specific shift that is occurring that's affecting all of us?

Laura Lyn: There has been unease since the earth opened and swallowed many of its children. The chaos and sadness with the wars of the people is also causing this uneasy feeling. The sensitive ones of the earth are feeling the unease; they are questioning their purpose and feeling much doubt and trepidation.

We are here to help you sustain and bring back the energy. Understand as individuals you can do little; however, with the power and light of our energies surging through you and collectively through the groups consciousness you can help bring light and peace. Trust our channel and our message.

Dale: Do you have anything else that you would like to tell us this evening?

Goddess Energy

Laura Lyn: Monica this message is for you. We will be here with you. We understand that you have a very stressful week ahead. The Goddess energy, a loving energy, a beautiful spirit of the feminine essence will be with you and her name is Mary. Mary will be with you to hold your hand throughout the day and you will feel her presence as you already did. She is bringing you great energy, love, inspiration and peace.

You will feel her presence tonight and throughout the week loving you and your children. She is here for you my dear.

Monica, this is Mary. I want you to know that I see the honor that you bring your children and the love that you bring to the world and I am here to tenderly help you through this process. I will hold your hand, I will guide you and I will help you sustain. I will bring you energy and peace. See the light energy flickering around you now. This is me and I am here for your peace. I love you and I will protect you.

Monica: Thank you. Is it time to wake Laura?

Laura Lyn: We have one more message.

Love is Always the Answer

Laura Lyn: We understand the weariness and the energy that is flowing in the room at this present moment. We are here to help guide you into a higher light. Remembering that love is always the answer and this has always been the truth that has been shared.

Feel the energy in the room right now. This is the love. Bring back the energy from the beginning. Allow the love to flow through, remembering the magic. Bask in this energy, this is truth. Feel the presence of spirit right now

∞ *The Spirit's Journey* ∞

moving through the voice and channel. This is love pure love unconditional. Feel the presence.

Dale: Thank you. I would like to ask that Laura's angels and guides bring her back to us. And we thank you for all the messages.

---

[1] Crown Chakra - *Sahasrara*, which means 1000 petal lotus, is generally considered to be the chakra of pure consciousness, within which there is neither object nor subject. Symbolized by a lotus with one thousand multi-colored petals, it is located either at the crown of the head, or above the crown of the head.

[2] Metatron - is considered one of the highest of the angels. Metatron is also referred to as the voice of God and the one who holds the scales of justice.

∞ Realm to Realm ∞

4-5-2011

Spirit Owl, Rudolf Steiner

∞

Laura Lyn: We are asking for light around all of us so that the highest greatest good, highest greatest light harmony and peace can come forward. Receiving clear messages, concise messages for those in need, we are asking for clarity and information to help bring us forward to a new place new light.

And we are asking the messages to come forward from those enlightened beings that are the highest greatest good, highest greatest light; only allowing these high vibrations to move forward and through the channel. And we are asking for protection.

And we are asking that you allow me to go to sleep while protecting me and that my voice be a channel to help bring peace. We are seeking universal messages to help those who are searching. Please allow me to go into a rested state where I can channel messages.

Dale: Who's with us this evening?

Laura Lyn: There are many. Spirit Owl is speaking presently.

Dale: What would you like to tell us this evening?

Patterns of Life

Laura Lyn: The pattern of life is moving forward in a place of distinction. Many are feeling certain doubt of their future; there will always be evolution of the spirit, so fear not, fear is the enemy.

∞ The Spirit's Journey ∞

Life is the manifestation of joy and peace, while bridging the pathway of love. We are here to discover together a truth. A truth that life within the human existence has the knowledge to bridge, the decision to move forward, and to ascend to a high perfected state, that state of unconditional love.

Understand that the path that friends and family deliver or walk upon is their own journey to discover their own truth, and the truth lies within that person; their perfected state.

The existence of the human race, the spirit, and the individual soul, is a beautiful plethora of energies and when you see the individual moving forward or even lowering their vibration you are seeing miracles at play. Life and all its existence is a miracle.

These are the lessons in life, the reflection of the existence where you can individually evolve yourself. So we invite you to watch and to grow accordingly. Thank you.

All: Thank you.

Shift

Stephanie: I sense a change for all of us, something around the corner. Almost like a higher plan. Do you have any words on that?

Laura Lyn: The world is moving forward in rapid cessation. There is a shift surely happening within our realm. If you are referring to the Northeastern Ohio region there are certain elements that are coming forward to help levitate or rather raise the vibration or frequency of truth.

So trust, have faith and continue the works through prayer and meditation. Remember that the highest light is in understanding that all pathways have purpose.

Dream World – Multiple Existences

Dale: Is Rudolph Steiner with us this evening?

Laura Lyn: Yes, speaking.

Dale: I would like to ask you about rebirth, or even a death of your previous self within one lifetime.

Laura Lyn: The realms within your own vibratory system move through many pathways. There are many lifetimes and life expansions within the facets of your being. There are many births and rebirths and many souls that are within the fractures of your system.

There are many dimensions within the soul. For instance in your dream work, your dream world state, you may be in the existence of two, three, five, seven, even ten human existences. As you develop through these existences, your higher self, your spiritual self, is gathering this information and your physical self here on Earth is growing at an expedited rate.

And just as the snake sheds and transforms, your soul transforms, splits, divides and moves forward in multi-faceted directions and helps to elevate others. So therefore Dale you are correct, there are many births and rebirths within the soul's single session and in this development of the soul level there are multi levels at any moment that you are living through.

∞ The Spirit's Journey ∞

Dream World - Counsel

Stephanie: I would like to know, who is actually talking to me at night in my sleep? Am I truly visiting another dimension in dreamtime?

Laura Lyn: You are with your counsel. You are truly in dream world. You are in a place where magic is becoming your truth, your honor, and your state. You are working with your counsel, your spirit guidance.

Stephanie: Thank you.

Releasing the Past

Dale: Many of us are attempting to release past trauma or conditioning. Is there anything you can tell us about release?

Laura Lyn: The release of toxicities within your system, within the cell, depending on your motive, is simply a direction of decision. Allow that decision to be made of release. It is that simple.

There are many tools that you can use to help alleviate this. We have instructed Laura in many of these tools such as planting the misdirected element; writing the information that you would like to release and planting into the earth.

Allow the earth to dispose of the element and the toxicity in her time and her manner. Allow the beauty of a plant to grow in its presence allowing the beauty to expand into the environment. Releasing the toxicity is essential however; it can only be made after the decision of release.

Love Light

Dale: And does anyone have anything else they would like to relay to us tonight?

Laura Lyn: Yes. Dale, you are beginning to see the true magic in your heart. You are beginning to see the light around you. You are seeing life for where it can go and the happiness that it can discover. Trust your path for you are where you truly belong. Question no more please, for just the mere questioning is lowering the vibration of this great truth.

Doubt is the darkness. We are here by your side and by your wife's side to help you gently move to a direction of helping many. The love that you have around you will sustain and grow.

Trust this magic, trust this light, you are at the epicenter of this light and we are so grateful that you have finally found home[1]. Thank you Dale.

Dale: Thank you. I would like to ask that the angels, guides, and enlightened beings help to wake Laura and bring her back to this space. Thank you for all the beautiful messages this evening.

---

[1] "We are so grateful that you have finally found home" - This is something that Laura said often as we were getting reacquainted almost two years before this message. *It does feel good to be home.* ~Dale

∞ Realm to Realm ∞
4-24-2011
Rudolf Steiner, Sylvia
∞

Laura Lyn: Thank you spirit guides and angels, thank you loved ones. I ask for Archangel Michael to come in to bring protection to the room, the home, surrounding us all with white light. Allowing only the highest greatest good, highest greatest light, highest greatest energies to come through to speak through me to bring forward messages that are helpful globally and direction to help bring forward peace and love.

We are going to ask for messages for Becky, Dale and Clara. We are going to ask for messages to help them on their life path.

Laura Lyn: There are three. I'm still kind of awake.

Dale: Which three are with us this evening?

Laura Lyn: We have Rudolph Steiner; there are two that are not ready to speak yet.

Dale: We can wait for them unless Rudolph has anything he would like to say.

See Beyond the Trees

Laura Lyn: Yes, thank you. While in the wilderness those that are unaware cannot see beyond the trees. Those who understand nature can see through and beyond every obstacle. These are my teachings.

There are obstacles, distractions, those things in life that we would like to avoid. But avoidance will only bring certain dissatisfaction in the life path for the meaning of life is to learn through these obstacles and find the strength within. There are many distractions in your life at this moment but they are rich in your destiny to realize.

Compassion is truth and must be learned for in that space true compassion will heal all wounds, disabilities, infringements, and intolerances. True compassion will bring forward courage and strength within your body, mind and soul, and will bring a new wisdom. Feel, see, understand, and look through the eyes of the other.

When there is pain there will be fear. When one brings out a poisonous or toxic effect, this makes the other recoil. It is often the fear within the initiator that expands into the other. That is a very uncomfortable feeling for then we must face our own fears that we may also lose control.

So tolerance and compassion is always the answer when faced with a difficulty of another person's behavior. Trust you have the wisdom to bring forward your heart to a compassionate resolution. This will bring honor to all. This is indeed what love is. Thank you.

All: Thank you.

Dale: Are the other two ready to speak or do you have more to say Mr. Steiner?

Breaking the Cycle

Laura Lyn: We see that our truths are being placed outwards and in this a vibration is being manifested. You will understand shortly that the truths unfold powerful insights that indeed change lives.

As you are teaching you are also learning and in that, building blocks of strength are surely delivered and built upon within your own structural walls. In this moment of gathering strength, the old poisons that are untruths and no longer necessary.

Trust the new direction that is being taught for this will bring a new truth to your life. This will indeed bring prosperity, abundance of resources and knowledge.

In this, my dear friend, your mission will be closely accomplished for we expect you to speak with your real voice and in this you will help the masculine energy be rebalanced.[1]

Again, part of the solution here is devoting to compassion while utilizing the masculine energy. In that balance you are internalizing love which will shape your future and your life. This will also alter your past pathway by increasing the vibration. This is actually altering the vibration of your ancestral root.

This is very exciting for you are breaking a cycle and releasing the past ill effects of what one may refer to as sin, missing the mark. This is very powerful work and we are very proud and honored that you have stepped forward dear friend.

Dale: Thank you. When I'm hearing these thoughts going through my head, am I hearing you speak to me or am I hearing my own truths?

Laura Lyn: You are hearing your higher voice, your higher truths. In that knowledge you are hearing the vibration of our direction infiltrating your auratic field[2]. Refer to that universal spirit, there is the knowledge, and it becomes internalized once you accept that you are worthy.

Spirit Guides – Earth Angel

Dale: Thank you. We have our friend Clara here tonight. Is there anything you have that you would like to tell Clara?

Laura Lyn: Thank you. Hello Clara.

Clara: Hello

Laura Lyn: You are a wise one. You have researched and known about our direction in your life since you were a young child. The angelic realm has always been very clear and near to you.

My name is Sylvia and I have been with you since you were a young child. And while this English name that I am bringing forward is not the name referred to me in the angelic realm, you have called me Sylvia since a young age. In fact you have known me for many lifespans.

I am here to remind you of my presence. I have loved you since you were born and before that point in time. You bring forward direction of healing and that presence of love to those you touch.

The energy that you bring forward with your craft, your art, your creativity, is always touching love. We enjoy working with you. We love you and we find strength, meaning our vibration quickens when working with a person who brings joy to this world.

∞ Realm to Realm ∞

We love you Clara and thank you. Understand that the smile on a face, perhaps a baby's face. The smile, joy, and happiness within that frame is where you find spirit.

The presence of spirit is everywhere. Look for joy and you will see us. You might get a quick glance, or internal vision, picture us through your mind's eye.

We will show you the direction and we will always bring you new direction. We are honored to work with you. We thank you and we love you.

Clara: Thank you

Laughter, Happiness

Dale: Yes, thank you. And we have Becky here. What would you like to say to Becky?

Laura Lyn: Hello Rebecca.

Becky: Hi

Laura Lyn: We are aware of your new belief and acceptance in yourself and this brings happiness to us. Your awareness of guidance has been opening and awakening. Truths are being revealed. There has been an internal shift that has taken place. With this you will feel what true joy is.

While the laughter has always been present and we are so aware of your healing affect with this, it is now time for you to realize the healing through your own self, through your own direction, through this awakening.

The laughter is wonderful, the joy though, the true joy is increasing within. You are increasing the vibration of the third eye within your system. Allow yourself to walk through that doorway of truth and belief.

Feel the subtle vibrations through the rocks, soils, trees and the leaves. Tap into all that nature reveals through the vibration. You will then feel this spirit at a stronger level.

Hold onto your thoughts when you have a suspicion that something is coming intuitively. Work through that source for you will bring healing. We thank you Rebecca for your appreciation and acceptance of this work.

Becky: Thank you.

The Earth - Spirit Rescue

Dale: Is there anything else you would like to tell us this evening?

Laura Lyn: We are hopeful that you remember the importance of bringing healing to the land, to the earth. Utilize every moment possible to bring healing to Japan. There are many souls who still are searching. There are souls we cannot reach, but those in the physical realm may be able to reach them.

We understand there will be a spirit circle soon. We request that you bring attention to Japan in this circle. There will be more consequential deaths through shocks and waves of bacterial infections. Please continue the prayerful mode to help these souls. Thank you.

Mound Builders in Ohio

Dale: Thank you. I am studying the mound builders in the Ohio region. Is there anything that you can tell us about their history?

Laura Lyn: The mound builders are the earth builders[3]. Their history goes back 14,000 years. It is very interesting when you realize that Peru, those at the current place of Peru, actually brought much influence to these lands 14,000 years ago.

The mounds were made for ceremonial reasons to lift up to the Gods, to continue the harvest, to continue the rains, to flourish the people, to give thanks. The conical growth, the height, was to go up to the Sun God to give ultimate thanks and to bury the dead, the eggs, and to bring forward honor. This was a nest building.

It was understood for safety and cleanliness that the dead must be bundled and buried. Many of the mounds included the dead. Just like ceremonies that you perform during a funeral, there was much grieving and blessing given to the family and village members of the clan. Within the burials were many beloved items, axes, tools, and jewelry, items for them to carry on into the next life.

There are many different tribes buried within these mounds. Many cultures were lost within history. Some will surface; some are completely lost.

We will bring forward a message of peace for the span of 4,000 years of the Pueblo tradition; peace was resonating deeply.

∞ The Spirit's Journey ∞

And in the serpents mouth it took upon an egg and life rejuvenates within, transition is formed, and life begins again. The story of the serpent and the egg is just as the story of Christ in the Christian religion. Life rises again. Thank you.

Dale: Thank you. We're getting to the limit of Laura's time. Is it a good time to wake her up?

Laura Lyn: Please

---

[1] Speak with your true voice – At this time I had a fear of speaking in a group. This fear is dissipating over time.

[2] Auratic Field – a field of subtle, luminous radiation surrounding a person or object. Sometimes it is said that all living things (including humans) and all objects manifest an aura. Some people can actually perceive the colors of different layers of the aura which are often associated with moods, health and personality traits.

[3] The mound builders are the Earth builders – were prehistoric inhabitants of North America who, during a 5,000-year period, constructed various styles of earthen mounds for religious and ceremonial, burial, and residential purposes.

∞ *Realm to Realm* ∞

4-26-2011

Rudolf Steiner

∞

Laura Lyn: Archangel Michael, I'm asking for a ray of light, a circle of light, to encircle this house, so only the highest greatest good, highest greatest light, highest greatest honor can come forward in the enlightened messages through spirit.

We are asking that the channels come through my voice, to work through me, through love. We are asking for clear messages. We would like to hear what you have to say and we are so grateful for this opportunity.

Dale: Who's with us tonight?

Laura Lyn: We have Rudolph Steiner

Dale: And what would you like to tell us tonight?

Shift - Awakening

Laura Lyn: There is much excitement in our travels and roads and with this enlightenment that is newly formed. We are at a time and place where the awakening is happening at a quickened state and this formation of spirit and light is at a place where mortals are receiving the energies and there is much confusion. We are here to help bring a message and it is needed for there will be those searching for direction.

The focal point is certainly love. This is the true message of the land, as Great Spirit has brought forward. The land is now at a place that is receiving light unadulterated from sadness, and fears.

∞ *The Spirit's Journey* ∞

The shift is truly happening at a quickened state and we are grateful those here are listening and the messages will be brought forward.

The message is simply a state of being in joy and peace. One with your sisters and your brothers connected to the full force of the power of God, the great creator.

We certainly seek, hear, and know the messages from that light source are here and present now. We are most grateful. Thank you.

Everyone: Thank you.

Glimpse of another Realm

Dale: Is there anything that you feel we should hear as a group or individually? Anything you would like to say?

Laura Lyn: There is a place where the rainbow moves. In this place the colors and tones gently cascade. The glistening fairies dance through the sky. The realms they are many, the division is none.

Understand the true windows, the spaces are here among everything; and as the windows open and the doorways welcome; you are joining together with energies of every level. We are here to greet you as you receive messages from the different spaces.[1]

Understand the space is here to help you move forward in the direction of true healing. We are here to move with you, to bring you the knowledge. Seek us and we will come through.

Dale: I've told most everyone here about a dream I had. I saw some form of luminescent energy. Are you aware of what I was seeing and why?

Laura Lyn: We are aware. You walked through a realm we were speaking of. You are here among the spirit energy. There are times when the energy is lower form and higher form and while the space is much cleansed, there are certainly times when the darkened energy must follow to help create the space of balance.

And as you release within the toxic mode in the cellular tissue you will be in that phase of certain releases.

And as your awakened self moves forward, you are aware of the energy facing you. Not attacking you, merely facing you. You are moving forward now, released from much toxicity. With this, a new clarification and compassion is moving forward. We are grateful that you are releasing the energy that was once weighing you down.

Physical, spiritual, emotional, and cellular memory is the source of ultimate creation.

And as that space comes forward in the future, in the distant future all will absorb for all is connected.

While this is very interesting it is also very serious. Understand that the soul that connects the source within is the ultimate energy that moves forward. The body is dust, it is merely dust. The cell within the total soul source is where the truth is and moves forward.

Dale: Thank you.

∞ The Spirit's Journey ∞

[1] *The morning before this session, I woke up and saw a hovering mass of energy that was about 6 feet off the floor. I just stared at it for a while. I thought I was just half asleep and my vision was blurred. After looking at this for a while I got out of bed while still looking at this mass of energy. I walked to the foot of the bed and it remained in place. The mass of energy looked like luminescent tubes with vibrant colors, it emanated a ringing sound, and a distinct glow. I studied it for a while and then went to tell Laura about what I had seen.* - Dale

∞ Realm to Realm ∞

5-2-2011

Rudolf Steiner, King David

∞

Laura Lyn: Enlightened beings, messengers please come forward to bring precise messages. Clara is here looking for insight from a message we received a little while back about King David. Please bring forward King David if possible, or a messenger, so we can receive the insight for the directions and the message that was brought forward before.

We are asking for any messages for the universal energy. I'm going to ask Dale and Clara both to ask questions trusting, knowing that all is at the highest greatest good, highest greatest light and highest greatest love.

We are asking for your protection Archangel Michael, for all of us, to shield us through this work. I'm being asked to hold the bible and open it up to the psalm 27. (movement, pages turning)

Dale: Who's with us today?

Laura Lyn: We have Rudolph Steiner.

Dale: Hello Mr. Steiner, what do you have to tell us today?

Love – Defeat Fear and Darkness

Laura Lyn: The world is in a recent triumphant space where the light shall shine as a beacon upon this earth however, many wars will follow. The truth is, this is a spiritual war and those who gather in churches are certainly feeling this presence.

∞ *The Spirit's Journey* ∞

Fear is what has been bred through wars and throughout history. So we ask you to eradicate this fear and bring love, the mighty sword of love through every direction, through your light and source. We ask the elders and the matriarchs[1] to come forward to bring the truth of love.

The idea, the consciousness behind this truth, the truth of love, will multiply as the groups gather. This is the reason the missions are so important and must move forward.

But be wary, do not allow your guards to fall. For there will be a resonance of darkness that will try to dispute the light and through these interruptions, the consequences, the tower may fall. So be prepared through your shield for the mighty love will win. It is up to you.

Dale: Do you have anything you could tell Clara to help answer her questions about King David?[2]

Beauty and Love of Oneness

Laura Lyn: Hello Clara. We are understanding your recent questions. You have a hollow feeling within. We will try to help unmask this feeling, this perception.

Understand that there is a gift within you. You have a wisdom that comes from ages past. The wisdom is marked, and through this beautiful space is truth. We align with this truth and understand that your true eager devotion for this pathway is blessed by your energy. For you have a certain strength and honor. And through this honor you are bringing protection.

Don't allow a certain darkness, the energies, to dampen or alter the path. For you are a matriarch, a true wise one.

Your ideas and directions are totally supported through your mission. We will be here to help you move forward.

Align yourself with an understanding and knowledge that you will pick up frequencies of those on the path who help, and those on the path that hinder. Trust your insight and bring it forward for the knowledge is needed to protect so that your mission can be brought forward to help people on the three levels.

We bless you and thank you. Also understand that you are protected and have a keen insight for you have a beautiful messenger that has been known for many years to hold a star, a beautiful star that they named David. The message here, dear one, is that your messenger will always be with you to protect you for through that insight of protection through the beloved beauty of David.

You have keen knowledge that will bring forward a blessing, for where you step the flowers open. The flowers demonstrate the beauty. The beauty and love of oneness, for the flower carry all over through the pollens and nectar. A sweetness that brings forward the honey, the sweetness that sustains life. Please understand that you help sustain life through your sweetness. We are honored to work with you.

Clara: Thank you

Truth of Love

Dale: From what I understand so far, everything is an aspect of, and an expression of consciousness and it's all intertwined and connected and it's all necessary. Is that correct?

∞ *The Spirit's Journey* ∞

Laura Lyn: Every aspect of life, every tune, fiber, and cell is the expression of the great creator, for it was his aspect; meaning the consciousness of awareness, of feeling, and touch. The particles touching is where it all began.

Certainly it is all derived by consciousness but understand that the mere word is a direction, a mask, for all is truth, truth of love. While there is darkness that is the opposite polar effect, this sustains the balance.

The words, the descriptions we have enfolding upon us in the past, written in the words, they are here to tell a story of the great creation, great creator, great spirit, and the truth is, all is one in this raptured energy, this loved one.

Dale: Thank you. Laura is becoming tired I'd like to ask her angels and guides gently wake her and bring her back to us. We thank you for all the guidance during this session. Thank you.

---

[1] Matriarch - A woman who is who is powerful within a family or organization.

[2] King David - The second king of the United Kingdom of Israel according to the Hebrew Bible and, according to the Gospels of Matthew and Luke, an ancestor of Jesus Christ through both Saint Joseph and Mary.

∞ Realm to Realm ∞

5-5-2011

Rudolf Steiner

∞

Laura Lyn: Angels, spirit guides, loved ones, messengers we are asking for a circle of protection around us, protecting us during this sleep trance session where we will be focusing on our future as a community and any other messages you would like to bring forward for the higher greater good, higher greater light.

Please allow my voice to be the channel for the messages that is clear and precise with direction and focus so we know where to go to help others.

Dale: I Laura ready to speak?

Laura Lyn: Yes she is.

Dale: Who is with us tonight?

Laura Lyn: We have Rudolph Steiner.

The Three Layers

Dale: Hi Mr. Steiner, do you have anything you'd like to tell us tonight?

Laura Lyn: You have a deep understanding and respect for the law of nature. What I am referring to is you are internalizing the truth of the perfect source and this is the moment of oneness, for this is where the creator gathered the strength to come forward.

Understand the three developments of body, mind and soul. There are many development phases and layers there upon. We would like to move forward with the essence of connection. How we are connected to all and all is connected to us, and the whole being, whole particle. This is precision.

Understand that solitude within the individual is also of the utmost importance. Oneness holds the principle for the individual in the soul pattern to the point of the spirited body where we are connected to the three layers that are spoken of often: the dead, the undead and the unborn.

Behold the Beauty

Dale: What about the history of our origins? Is there anything you would like to add that you didn't add when you were here?

Laura Lyn: We have a cycle that is so imperative to understand. The soul wonders why there is darkness and light when the pain and confliction is rampant upon the heart level. And the truth is the experience of pain through the darkness, once interwoven and spoken through, won through resiliency and strength, becomes anew and this is where the light filters through.

The experience of the darkness is a large and wonderful gift. For once you walk through those doorways and hit your face upon the light after trudging through the darkened spaces, you are in a rapture and once again become anew.

The cycles are necessary for remembering the pathways from the past, from the fractures of the past experiences of lives gone by. Every person who has evolved into this worldly space has felt and known great evil and great love.

Every person who has evolved into this worldly space has seen much darkness and much light.

The cycle within the sphere of the soul child is diligent and knows truth. The insightful one will move forward understanding the law. The law is that the natural self beholds the beauty. The natural self is the spirit that the divine order has created. Thank you.

Atlantis – Secrets of the Past

Laura Lyn: There is a mass land, a land that has been uncharted. There is a land that will be discovered underneath the sea. This land has and will be a crystalline village where the modern man as you know it will learn the secrets of the past; the past that has been all but forgotten. Within the grids of the crystals, and within the geometric obelisk, there are many power surges and sources that will come forward.

You may have heard of this as Atlantean or Atlantis. It will be discovered on your calendar in 12 years and in that precise moment time will change. It will change rapidly. There will be need to learn these ancient ways and sacred ways. We invite you to understand and learn the history that is restored. The pathways of the geometric cone are impressive and will show an efficient manner where power in the future may be brought forward to help bring in an existence, comfort, and needed resources to help them on their path. There is need to discover these paths. There will be many resources that will come forward and realign human existence with these truths.

Dale: Thank you. We are also curious about our roots in Atlantis. What can you tell us about that?

Laura Lyn: There has been much interest and talk of Atlantis. While there is mere speculation on this planet for much of what is spoken of Atlantis is pure folklore from that imaginative space.

The truth is that Atlantis once was a people that were very conflicted. At one point Atlantis was split by greed. There was also a purified simplified people of Atlantis. The pure essence gave them great strength for they touched onto the sphere of the sky, winds, earth, stars, lunar and the solar energies.

The Atlanteans held the power within beautifully through their pure essence and belief. However, there was a split. There was a side that became jealous and envious for they did not behold this power to the same extent. They found their selves wanting to become more powerful and found a way to tap into a darkened energy to exploit the power.

While the energies of Atlantis were split there was also much rooted energy within the ancestry line. Therefore, as the great flood came and the land sank to the bottom of the sea there were many who escaped and found their selves on boats and crafts, floating devices, hitting other areas of the world. They moved forward and populated the lands.

Virtually every country in this world is touched with Atlanteans energy and every friend you behold has the spirit of the Atlantean within them either through their ancestry line or through their fractures of the soul line. However, understand that this means that they have either the side of the light or the dark. They have a shadow self-confliction or the light beholding energy.

This is where we have always taught that the ego must be checked for this is the darkest energy, the most damaging ascent. And when the ego is misdirected, the damage can move forward in a quickened state that can hurt many and be contagious.

Everyone: Thank you.

Christ Light

Dale: Mr. Steiner, in studying your works, I've realized the Christ light is very important. How can that be relayed in a neutral way. (*Without organized religious connotations*)

Laura Lyn: The Christ light is a concept meaning the light within. Christ consciousness is a high value of truth. I may be over sensitive on this matter for I teach and have knowledge that the Christ light is deep within us all, everyone, and the process is touched through every living being on this earth.

So understand this is a deep truth, not a religion, not dogma[1]. Research the Christ light and the truth, not only through my works, and you will see the answers within. Do you understand?

Dale: Yes, thank you. Is there anything else you would like to say?

Laura Lyn: Love is your ministry and there is no fault in that. We hope that you do not fear the connotation of this being a ministry.

∞ *The Spirit's Journey* ∞

And for those who it resonates with will capture that Christ light, love centered heart and move forward with this mission. For the world they need this truth and word. The world they need this light and love. The world they need this balance, harmony, and space; and they must move through; for there will be a time when the darkness will cascade its light. During this time it will bring confliction. It will falter and it will imitate.

The true Christ Light must come forward to shed the light on the darkness. False witnesses will become abundant so there will be a tremendous need for this ministry to move forward and the time is now. So please move forward.

Dale: Thank you. Is it ok for us to wake up Laura?

Laura Lyn: Please.

Dale: I would like to ask that Laura's angels and guides wake her, gently bring her back to us, and if possible give her a boost of energy as she comes out of this. And I want to thank you Mr. Steiner for all the messages tonight.

---

[1] Dogma - A doctrine or a corpus of doctrines relating to matters such as morality and faith, set forth in an authoritative manner by a church.

∞ Realm to Realm ∞

5-10-2011

Jophiel, Rudolf Steiner, Spotted Owl

∞

Lost loved one

Laura Lyn: Spirit Guides, Angels, Guided Ones, Archangel Michael we are asking for your total protection and light during this process of the sleeping trance. We are asking for clear messages for Cheryl, Clara, Jessica, Becky and Dale. We move forward in a place of love and light. Asking these messages come from a place of harmony and peace. Thank you Spirit.

Dale: Who is with us this evening?

Laura Lyn: Laura Lyn: We have three universal energies. The light wave Jophiel is present[1]. We have Rudolph Steiner, and Spotted Owl.

Dale: We have Clara's sister Cheryl with us what do you have to say to her?

Laura Lyn: Hello Cheryl

Cheryl: Hello

Laura Lyn: We are meeting you today and we would like to welcome you. We have spoken with your sister and her beautiful energy. We are understanding that you had a recent loss and this is a transitional time for you, a new beginning. And your husband would like to bring forward the following message:

Dear Cheryl, I love you like the day I met you. The emerald is cherished and so is the ruby. Please wear the emerald and ruby so I can communicate with you stronger. The green signifies the healing that you are still witnessing and going through and the red signifies the love I have for you.

You are as beautiful as the day I met you and you are very intelligent. I love you and I am so proud of you and I thank you; for you have helped me evolve to a space where I am so comfortable.

You have taught me love and I will forever be grateful. You have taught me that love is the most important emotion that one could carry. You are strong, fearless and devoted to your family and friends, forever loyal. I am proud that I was your husband; that I am your husband.

And please know that when it is your time I will be holding my hand out to you and we will have this life again. Both in the spiritual realm and in the physical space we will come back and meet again. For I have already seen this written for our future. I love you.

Laura Lyn: Cheryl?

Cheryl: Yes?

Message from Jophiel

Laura Lyn: You are a devoted soul. My name is Jophiel, and I have worked with you and brought you much energy of visions. I have brought you more presence, your ideas, your creative responses, arts, crafts, your friends, your family how you work with them through the creative resource. I will always be with you to help you in your future. I love you unconditionally. You have the gift of seeing. Do you see my spirit now?

Cheryl: No

Laura Lyn: Look closely dear one, the blue rays, when you see the blue lights and the blue rays, there I am. Hold onto that light. Know that I am always here. You may capture it out of the corner of your eyes, or as a shadow you may have already seen it. I am honored to work with you. Thank you.

Dale: What else do you have to tell us this evening?

Embracing Love

Laura Lyn: We are all present to bring forward a message. It is time now (thunder) to understand as the storms move into your life those are opportunities to see a new direction, to work through the present challenge. Embrace the challenge, and you are embracing the truth; for the darkness will never want you to move forward. It will want you to stop.

The light exists. See the beauty of the light always. Remind each other that the light is always at the present. And as this energy shapes forward, comes forward, know that is where the love energy infiltrates the heart. Light is love, love is light. Embrace that light and you are embracing love.

Move forward in the direction where love is at the center, loving people for where they are and who they are. This is the direction of insight and truth. As the spirit speaks, a new direction of light is coming forward that is working with all. However, only a certain type of individual can truly understand and focus on this light. Those will be coming forward that are searching. Thank you.

Clara: This is Clara, are there any messages you have for me tonight?

Ministry – Helping

Laura Lyn: Hello Clara, our friend. We are delighted you are here tonight. And we are hopeful that you understand that there was direction and clear sign that you are on the right pathway with your ministerial position that focuses on the insight that you have received many years ago.

You will have a special purpose within your ministry and with this a calling. We hope you understand that you will be visiting those in the hospital that are sick bringing blessing, prayer, and laughter; a healing presence. Does this feel comfortable to you Clara?

Clara: Yes.

Laura Lyn: We would also like you to visit the aging in nursing homes or children at the hospital. Does this resonate with you Clara?

Clara: Yes .

Laura Lyn: Thank you.

Clara: Thank you.

Laura Lyn: We are delighted that you have heard this pathway. This is a gift you will be bringing the future ministry. We are here with you and will always follow you and walk beside you. The blessing of your presence will be noted and will bring a certain harmony and peace to the ones that you are visiting. We thank you.

Clara: Thank you.

The Fire Keeper

Becky: I'm curious about my past lives, who I've been and how they relate to who I am today?

Laura Lyn: We are so grateful you came forward with this question. There is a true connection with the group. For you were a Native American along with the clan. One called the fire keeper. The fire keeper may have been one that could have felt left out or not important.[2]

The truth is that the village came forward and honored the fire keeper, for the fire keeper was the one who always brought the substance, the heat, the warmth. Without the fire keeper the foods could not be cooked, the people could not be warm, the water could not be boiled, and one could not cleanse. So we honor the fire keeper.

Relating this to your life now in the present moment, it is your position to bring fire substance to your new work. You name was Little Buffalo with the Sioux, your name is now Rebecca and the fire must burn to bring your works forward for the future.

If you allow the flame to go out your pathway will be blocked. Open up the fire. Keep the logs upon the fire. The fire and the smoke must work together to bring forward the truth of the pathway. The smoke represents the cleansing; the fire represents the heat, the initiative.

∞ *The Spirit's Journey* ∞

You will have many responsibilities within the work that you bring forward in your future pathway. It is your job now to ask the fire to grow and to compound and to keep balanced. Thank you Rebecca.

Becky: Thank you.

Dale: If Laura is not too depleted I would like to give you this opportunity to bring forward whatever you would like to say.

Message from the Lumerians

Laura Lyn: We are here to bring forward the message of hope and grace. We have brought forward a message that will help transcend time. Our direction is to bring forward love. We are here to make sure that the message of love multiplies and assimilates all levels of the spheres.

We are the Lumerians and we bring forward the message of hope and freedom. We are here to help bring forward the message. We have lost the message in the past, and now it is time to bring forward the direction again. We will bring forward this message in the future.

Hold on to its light so that you can move forward. We are here to say thank you for hearing our direction. We will continue to work with your workforce. We are here to help deliver this message. You have evoked our energy accordingly and we thank you.

Dale: Thank you.

Everyone: Thank you.

Dale I would like to ask that the guides, angels, and enlightened ones help to wake Laura and bring her back to us and give her some energy that may have been taken in this process if you can; and we thank you for the messages.

---

[1] Light Wave Jophiel - We found it interesting that Jophiel is referred to as the light wave.

[2] Fire keeper - An honored tribal member who made a solemn commitment to ensure that the sacred flame, a source of light, heat and energy, would always be kept burning.

∞ *The Spirit's Journey* ∞

∞ Realm to Realm ∞

5-11-2011

Spotted Owl, Hannah

∞

Some friends made an appointment to ask Laura health related questions while she's in sleep trance.

Laura Lyn: Thank you for bringing that light and the love and I'm asking for a veil of protection around each one of us during this trance channeling message. I'm asking that your beautiful ray of light flows around each one of us and that we are protected through the messages. I'm asking the messengers, loved ones, the guided ones for clear concise messages that will help everybody. We will be researching today if it is possible for a guide to come through with the information we are seeking. And we are thanking you for this time we have together respectfully.

Dale: Who's with us this evening?

Laura Lyn: We have Spotted Owl and Hannah.

Dale: What would you like to tell our group tonight?

Balance and Restoration

Laura Lyn: We have been excited to see the direction of change that is happening upon this earth and the movement that is bringing forth great change, great direction into the fourth world dimension. This is now happening at an unprecedented space and time; meaning that the rates of challenges that have been taking place upon this world are now coming to a place of resolution.

The earth, she is claiming her substance and this is bringing happiness to the universe. You have seen many tragedies upon recent times and this is certainly very impressive and unsettling. But we promise this is about balance and restoration and will hold great truth for the future. This earth may and must sustain; people in the indigenous truths are again being revealed.

The world they are hearing the beginnings and the simplicity and getting into the root. This makes our people happy. We are blessed that you are moving forward in the direction that has been called upon many years ago.

We will work beside you and walk beside you in this great destiny. We are honored to be here in this space with you. Thank you.

Dale: Thank you. Is there anything you would like to tell Nicole?

Trust the Wolf

Laura Lyn: Nicole I have Gray Wolf[1] present. You have been followed by the wolf throughout your life. At about age 10 you started hearing voices, seeing shadows, hearing different dimensions, and the wolf followed you to bring great protection.

This wolf will carry you protection and bring a place of independence while working within the planned destiny. Trust the wolf. The den leader, the matriarch of the wolf clan is very protective indeed as you are. Wolf medicine carries wisdom.

Honor the wolf during the full moon and the new moon. Carry the wolf spirit outdoors and honor her, the she-wolf, the feminine aspect and glory. As the wolf foot pad walks on the earth in beauty this you must honor also. Thank you.

Nicole: Thank you

Dale: We got together tonight to ask some questions about improving health what could you tell us about that?

Health – weight loss

Laura Lyn: We are here bringing forward messages that will help bring forward a metabolism change for those searching in a safe orient. Flushing out the bodily cell is imperative. Reaching the toxicity of the trauma and the emotion and any imbalances that are brought on the body.

We are asking to flush out the system by drinking plenty of water and bringing into your system a compound of bromelain[2], papain[3] and green tea[4].

The enzyme bromelain will help bring the fats to the surface of the cell so they can readily release.

The papain enzyme will help bring balance and restoration and the green tea will help flush the toxicities with a mild thermogenic[5] action through the system.

We also want to explain that many women in the room have hormone deficiency that is causing weight gain. Estrogen overload is apparent. Estrogen is found in soy and in milk and dairy products. And the antigens are attaching to the receptors imitating feminine estrogen through the system.

Natural progesterone is very helpful to bring the metabolism back. We request 2000 milligrams of fish oil,

500mg of Vitamin C, 400 IUE's of Vitamin E, and 80mg of pycnogenol[6]. And adding the regimen of the bromelain and papain will also benefit the metabolism.

Dale: Does anyone else have a question?

Nicole: You suggested the fish oil. Do you have an alternative for a vegetarian?

Laura Lyn: Yes, flax seed oil is sufficient.

Nicole: in the same amount?

Laura Lyn: we request 1000mg.

Nicole: Thank you

Dale: Is there anything else you would like to say to us this evening?

The Universe Depends on Mother Earth

Laura Lyn: We see the beauty, the sky, the earth. It is so important to keep this space clean. It is important to be diligent with this message and to carry the message to the future children.

We are a proud people and we still walk upon this earth as if it's our own, as it was. We ask, we beg that you please bring forward the message to help keep the Mother clean.

Mother Earth brings so much in her blossoms, her trees, her rivers, and brother sky, and the winds, upon the Mother. The universe depends upon the Mother so we all depend upon you to keep her clean and safe. Thank you.

Dale: Thank you

Everyone: Thank you

Hormones - Bioengineered foods

Nicole: I have a question about the hormones. Are the hormones that are affected is it because of the meat we've been eating?

Laura Lyn: As we stated it is within the dairy products and yes, you are correct it is in the meats. It is virtually in every substance and every food. There is a new process that is happening within the food system.

Bioengineered foods[7] complicate a system and soys are being represented in every sub food system. What we refer to as sub food is not the chain that your body is readily accustomed to. The foods you are now eating and are entering the body are laced with soy. Soy replicates hormones that are within your system and then you have estrogen overload. It is imperative that this becomes balanced or there will be many women, young women having heart attacks, strokes and thyroid issues.

And then there is another issue that is happening at rapid cessation. The true iodine is not the same as it once was and this is causing problems in some parts of the country and many women are having the thymus gland swollen and the thyroid itself swells. And when the swelling and the inflammation takes place the thymus and the thyroid cannot work with the endocrine system correctly and this releases not only toxics in the system and the *glycemic* raise to heighten response; in this takes place in the system, which they refer to as fight or flight. Eventually the metabolism slows or rises depending on your personal chemical makeup.

So there is a third issue underlying where there is a place where the woman who are receiving messages through the spirit world are utilizing bodily organs that are very difficult to manipulate and this is causing an influx in the system. Now this also happens to men however, women have the compounding issues with hormonal response. Men's metabolism is naturally so much more quickened.

Ascending Together

Laura Lyn: We have one more message. We are here to say thank you. We know there are many in the room that are actively seeing spirits, and feeling their presence and opening the doors. Everyone in this room believes and is aware of the presence of spirit. Understand that the spirit energy is here to help. We want to help the world and its children.

We are here to help ascension, the movement of higher energy, the higher frequency the higher light. This helps us move forward and ascend. We are here to help you, but please help us. Be truthful, be honest. Be free. Be in harmony and peace. Be loving. Be grateful. Be in heaven. For this is the heaven sphere.

The angels will carry you and bring you flight. We will wrap our wings around you and bring you glory. We'll be with you when there is sadness. The inspiration that flows forward is surely our voice. Honor our voice. Be in thanks. Allow the presence of spirit to move forward. We are here to raise the vibration of love. Blessings and light dear children. Thank you.

Everyone: Thank You.

Ask and Believe

Becky: Before we bring Laura back is Raphael present?

Laura Lyn: Yes, surely

Becky: While you have Laura in your care, can you possibly give her some type of healing so these sessions don't totally deplete her? Could you kind of restore her energy and just work with her so that she's just not so drained?

Laura Lyn: Thank you for asking. As is taught *simply ask and believe* and there it is.

Becky: Thank you.

Dale: I'd like to ask that the angels and enlightened beings bring Laura back to us gently. We are asking that you give her some healing energy as she comes out of her trance and that she come out of it energized and awake. We thank you and honor you for all of the messages.

---

[1] Gray Wolf – Native American Spirit Guide.

[2] Bromelain – is extracted from the stems of pineapples. It has a history of folk and modern medicinal use. As a supplement it is thought to have anti-inflammatory effects.

[3] Papain – enzyme used in the care of some chronic wounds to clean up dead tissue, found in digestive enzyme mixtures, and meat tenderizer.

[4] Green tea - Green tea contains carotenoids, tocopherols, ascorbic acid (vitamin C), minerals such as chromium, manganese, selenium or zinc, and certain phytochemical compounds. It is a more potent antioxidant than black tea, although black tea has substances that green tea does not such as theaflavin.

[5] Thermogenic - Thermogenic means tending to produce heat and is commonly applied to drugs which increase heat through metabolic stimulation.

[6] Pycnogenol - an antioxidant which is an extract of maritime pine bark or grape seeds. Studies show that the antioxidant capabilities of pycnogenol are 20 times more powerful than vitamin C and 50 times more potent than vitamin E. The active ingredients found in French maritime pine bark and grape seed extract work directly to help strengthen all the blood vessels and improve the delivery of oxygen to the cells.

[7] Bioengineered foods

5-25-2011
Rudolf Steiner, Raphael
∞

Laura Lyn: We are asking for protection and light around this home, around all the peripheral. We are asking that any lower vibrations that are in this house right now must be released to harm none. And only the highest consciousness of light through the Christ light, through the highest ascensions are here present and welcome.

We are asking that high energy, that high light, to come forward to bring the messages. We are so grateful for your energy and your guidance and we are welcoming this guidance tonight to receive answers to our questions. If you could just allow me to drift off that so I can speak your messages clearly and concisely. Thank you spirit.

Mirror, Reflect and Internalize

Dale: Can you tell us what is essential in life?

Laura Lyn: All are present to hear the good news that freedom, true freedom is brought forward through love. We honor love. We honor culture. We honor the earth and all its great people.

All have an opportunity to find ascension through self-realization. As one taps into the great Christ consciousness internally, the ascension will follow. This is necessary so that the levels, those that are seen and unseen, can also mirror, reflect and internalize the great truths of honor, love, harmony and peace; the truth of God's grace.

∞ The Spirit's Journey ∞

The great creator brought forward the human essence and spirit. And in that perfection there is a connection to every source particle. Through that essence nature nurtures within the roots of the earth. The truth is revealed.

Within the planetary cycle the truths are categorized and set into motion. The frequencies and information you are receiving are through this categorized library of information that started thousands of years ago at the great beginnings.

The cycles are churning quickly and will be revealing a new era of distinction. The era of distinction that we are speaking of is a revelation of truth. At this moment the revelation is peaking and in that splintered second, minute time, sparks of energy are forming on the planet earth where simplicity and agility are blending.

The simple message of truth and love and the agile frequency, the quickened state is forming. The messages are coming clear and quickened, precise; and through this point of precision, love is being honored. The love we speak of is internal, that of a Mother and Father.

The Great Father, Great Spirit allows this love to be personified through the mother and father so that you can get a minute understanding of the love and devotion that the Great Creator has for all the people for all the children.

The Christ consciousness is here as the son to teach that the love is obtainable by all. The Mother, the Earth, is here to nurture that love. So there you have Father, Son and the Holy Spirit. The Mother and the Sisters are the winds. The Brothers are the distinction between day and night.

We are revealing great truths for you to share and to behold. We seek for this foundation to be a fountain of knowledge that will help bring forward a new day.

We hope that the messages are clear and concise. We urgently would like you to move forward with helping those that cannot help themselves. Help those that are incarcerated and have intolerances within their own lives. They can't find their own truth. We will bring and gather much strength to help you move forward with helping the children, helping the community, helping the reservation.

Dale: Thank you. These things are happening very quickly. Is there anything you can tell me about focus? Focus is very difficult right now.

Living What You Know

Laura Lyn: It would be very difficult, for you are trying to understand the concepts, but what we ask is that you internalize through faith and understanding that the presence is all around you.

Tapping into this joyfully is the answer Dale, tapping into it joyfully, finding that inner heart, inner love, inner compassion. You have read so much, you have studied so many words, and you already have the knowledge.

Now it's time to bring forward the information into your heart, by breathing it in, deep breathing. Acknowledgement to spirit; acknowledgement to that inner light. You are that light. You are that inner love. You are harmony and peace.

∞ *The Spirit's Journey* ∞

You bring forward that love internally through that Christ consciousness of perfection. That perfection is unconditional love. Breathe in the love. Breathe in the light. Honor that light. Understand, that light is Great Spirit shining internally.

Bring that internal light externally to show the love, show the harmony, and show the peace. That is the acknowledgement. That is when you understand completely, that this is truth. Allow it to shine brightly to the world, you are that light, you are that love. Do you understand?

All is connected. All is righteous. All is truth

Dale: I am studying the development of the angels and archangels. I would like to show how that development goes hand in hand with people. Is that important for us to understand?

Laura Lyn: It is your personal quest to understand the embodiment of ascension. However, when we speak of simplicity we are putting in the forefront the great truth of ascension of spirit, the light, the energy.

When one is in a place of light, they allow this light to shine through the heart chakra and it reaches people. They feel it and they personify it. They understand it, and it captures their heart, this in turn brings them an internal mission: to reach for higher places in their life.

However, there may be a certain lot that may be interested in the levels and the history of ascension but please understand that this is a theory; a theory that was brought forward through the ages for mortal man to understand.

It is like all an illusion of sorts for truth is that connection, all connection webs and weaves to a place where there really are no true levels. For one depends on the other to grow so therefore it is my impression and opinion that the levels that were written, over complicates a simple truth: All is connected. All is righteous. All is truth. We are sorry if this disappoints.

Mirror Love

Dale: No, I think that's beautiful. Would you say that the importance of love is that we mirror that out to the world and its mirrored back to us because we are all connected and we are all one?

Laura Lyn: Absolutely, and when looking at the illustration that you were learning from my works, I think it was of an extreme importance for you to see the analytical persuasion; for the way your mind works, you have an inert need to understand on the deepest level why an action and reaction is significant and bares truth.

You certainly do not want to walk into any direction and be fooled. So the personal quest was necessary for the lines, the directions, and the ascension graph you needed to understand all the connections. And for your quest I am glad it was written that way. Do you understand?

Dale: Yes, it is absolutely perfect for what I needed to know. I think this conversation today is clearing things up for me. I've felt like ok, I've got this but what exactly should I do now?

∞ The Spirit's Journey ∞

Raphael - A Healing

Laura Lyn: We invite you this precise moment, if you are interested, to receive the light that helps bring a quickened healing through the heart, a spiritual awakening. The same spiritual awakening you had the first time you spoke to Laura. Do you remember?

Dale: Yes

Laura Lyn: Well we are inviting you this precise moment to receive an altered and aligned, elevated ascension through the heart chakra. Are you willing and ready?

Dale: Yes.[1]

Laura Lyn: Please take a deep breath.

My name is Raphael and I am here to bring forward a healing. The healing will go forward through your heart chakra.

Please lay down. Take a nice deep breath. Imagine your breath is moving in and out of your heart. With each breath, breathe, allowing the air to come through and flow through.

Breathe in my beautiful green light. Breathe in the word harmony. Allow this light to shine and brighten with each breath. Now with this breath elevate the heart to the word love.

Take a nice deep breath and feel the love purging every cell in your body. Release the toxicities now through your breath.

The feeling of insignificance, release it now.

The feeling of fear, release it now.

The feelings of dread release it now.

The feeling of uncertainty, release it now.

Now witness the light that is shining above you and moving into your heart. Feel this light well within your heart chakra and move through your body.

With it, with every heartbeat, love shining.

With every heartbeat, love shining.

Receive the love that is universal; that is conscious; that wants to bring forward change to the world; that wants to bring forward beauty to the world. This beauty, this light brings with it tolerance, patience, guidance, harmony and peace.

This light holds wisdom.

Breathe in the light and manifest the love.

With this light a new maturing will take place. Breathe in this energy. Allow the energy to flow through every cell. Allow the energy to manifest within every cell. The light will be attracted to more light. The love will attract more love. The harmony will attract more harmony.

Hold this torch; allow it to shine; for this is the Christ consciousness that wells within. Now take another deep breath allow the cords of love to fill you deeply. I will come back at any time that you seek my assistance to help you. You may communicate with me directly. I will always be here when you ask. Do you understand?

Dale: Yes, thank you.

∞ The Spirit's Journey ∞

(waking Laura)

---

[1] Raphael Healing - Laura's voice changed somewhat during this healing. I was taken by surprise here. I copied this recording to my phone and listened to this section many times throughout the following months while falling asleep.

∞ Realm to Realm ∞

6-13-2011

Rudolph Steiner, Edgar Cayce, Raphael, Chief Two Feathers and Chief White Feather

∞

Laura Lyn: Thank you guides and messengers and loved ones. We are asking for a veil of protection around the home around every one of us during this sleep trance session. We have Jan and Jessica, Laura, Dale, Jason and Becky here and if there are individual messages to come forward for them they are welcomed. We are asking for clear, concise messages for us as individuals and also for the center and any global messages that would be helpful for people to hear or listen to, read.

We are grateful for everything that is coming forward, Thank you. Asking for Archangel Michael to come forward and bring a shield of protection around all of us.

Dale: is Laura ready to speak?

Laura Yes.

Dale: Who is with us tonight?

Laura Lyn: There are many present tonight. There is a support system here and ready to talk to speak; Rudolph Steiner, Edgar Cayce, Raphael, Chief Two Feathers and Chief White Feather.

Dale: Thank you. Jason has a question for you.

Past Lives - Current Life Purpose

Jason: What is my proper place in this world?

∞ The Spirit's Journey ∞

Laura Lyn: Jason, you have seen me in your dreams. You have spoken to me and you have heard me. I am your brother from many moons ago. You know me as Chief White Feather and you were a great warrior in our clan. You were also a great animal healer. You spoke to the animals, you helped them heal and that healed our friends and our woods and our trees and it moved forward.

We expect you will once again work with the animals, help them heal, communicate with them. You carry your mother's gift although you carry it more precisely with the creatures of this world. You understand the animals.

This is why you enjoy music because it's a way to communicate vibrationally for the birds, the feathered ones to hear the flute. It speaks to the birds. The drum speaks to the turtles. In the future you will be talking to those on the floor of the forests and to the ones in the sky with the pipes. You are healing the animals with your music.

When you hold an animal they understand your energy; they trust you. They know you will not hurt them. Always honor these creatures for they are much wiser and older than any human on this earth. Move forward with your gift and in the future you will be a well-known communicator. Learn from those around you for they are wise.

You will be able to have a very reputable business if you wish working with the animals for there are people who are searching for information about their pets and you will be able to interpret what the animal is saying, where they are hurting, where they are in chaos from the past and help release that sadness if they were abused.

Trust your mission for this as a blessing. I will always be here for you for I am your brother. You have brought our family much pride. Your skin may not be red in the present day but we will always look at you as not a pale face but as a clan member that we hold with much pride.

We salute and hold great pride toward you our brother. You are on a good path. We are proud that you have lost the need for anger and hostility. There is no purpose in this life to hold that, to hold such emotion for this hostile place in the present life will only land you in a place of not holding freedom.

You are much better suited to work at a zoo or a place where they take care of wild animals than being behind bars. So please hold your tongue, your anger, for it is not for this world. And walk with honor for you were a warrior, you saved our land and today you are a warrior for the animals and you will help save their lives. Thank you for being here.

Dale: Thank you. Is there anything you would like to tell us this evening?

Great Source of One

Laura Lyn: We are here together as a group, a counsel. At this moment the counsels are bridging. We are here to help you help others. This is our whole reason for existence is to help. When we are able to bridge and help a human find their space of existence, their reason for life, we are embracing this moment; for we are also celebrating

∞ *The Spirit's Journey* ∞

our energy. When that happens, that great source of one becomes a little stronger, a little wiser.

You see, when we are here to help you, and when you receive this help, you are able to help others; that strengthens source. Once that happens the source is able to help more through bringing forward this energy to the lines of consciousness.

As individuals in this room everyone has had a calling to help embrace others so in turn you are our counsel and we are your counsel. We work here together collectively to help others enrich and rise. Everybody here in this room has been charged to help bring energy to others in their own unique way through your talents and skills.

You have all been here before, you have been here in the past together; you will be together in the future. The group that you are with currently is your family, your friends. You are able to help each other evolve and in that space you will help others.

Please understand that everybody together is connected for a reason. There is a beautiful picture that we see in this space. We are so grateful of the eager energies that have been brought forward to help spread our message. We will be here to help you help others. Thank you.

Everyone: Thank you

Dale: Do you have more that you would like to say?

Laura Lyn: We feel that we are finished. Thank you.

Dale: We thank you for everything and we'll all do our best with everything. I would like to ask that you gently

∞ Realm to Realm ∞

help to wake Laura up and give her some energy if you can as she's waking up. We thank you for the messages.

∞ *The Spirit's Journey* ∞

∞ Realm to Realm ∞

7-7-2011

Handriel, Spirit Guide Red Fox
∞

This is a private life path session for Rhonda.

Laura Lyn: Archangel Michael thank you for bringing protection around Rhonda[1], Dale, and I. We are asking for a spirit circle of protection. We are asking during this time for this sleep trance that the elders, angels, guides, and loved ones come through very clearly and concisely and that this is for the highest greatest good, highest greatest light and highest greatest honor.

We are very grateful for this time and this opportunity to bring forward spirit messages, soul path messages for Rhonda. We are asking that Rhonda's guides and those influencing her life on a spiritual level come through to bring forward messages that will help her on her life path and her destiny.

We are very grateful for the time that we have together. And as I go to sleep, I am asking that I am totally protected in your light and love. So let it be.

Dale: Is Laura ready to speak?

Laura Lyn: She is ready.

Dale: Thank you. Who is with us tonight?

Laura Lyn: We have two messengers. One angelic influence named Handriel, and we have Red Fox[2], who is a spirit guide, a Cherokee.

Dale: What would you like to tell Rhonda this evening?

∞ The Spirit's Journey ∞

Bring Beauty to this Earth

Laura Lyn: I have been with you since before you were born to this world, to this earth plane. I have watched you grow and been pleased to see such spirit energy from the heart, such dedication walking in beauty, understanding that your light is moving, and bringing beauty to this earth, to the people of the earth.

We have been very pleased. For your journey, while it has turned complicated is still certainly diligently moving forward for your ministry, your truth, and your light. We will continue this step with you for we see that the dedication will bring a beautiful manifestation of love and this is truly the focus of this lifetime journey with you and for you.

Trust your movement. We are dedicated to walk in this journey with honor. We thank you.

Remember Hearing the Spirit Within

Rhonda: Would you be able to share about my soul's plan? What experience was I supposed to get over the tragic loss of both my sister and brother in this lifetime?

Laura Lyn: Yes my dear we understand your question fully and we would like to bring you back to that moment, that loss. You were desperately searching for answers and seeking direction and we were there beside you certainly.

The Dead, the Undead and the Unborn

We understood the purpose; for we understood that you had a connection, a certain connection that is very beautiful and honored to transcendence. This does not come quickly, easily, or without pain. However; it does come with many blessings to behold to the earth, to the hemisphere, to the space of the three levels: the dead, the undead and the unborn.

You were preparing at that tragic moment to help other family members in the future. We would like you to entertain or put some energy toward the thought of helping, possibly with fundraising, or working in the field of transplant, or you may have already have worked with the hospice development, helping people transfer to this space of light.

This is critical work that is needed for those who have the utmost understanding about spirit and light, for you speak to spirit, do you not? Do you Rhonda remember hearing the spirit within?

Rhonda: Yes.

Laura Lyn: This is a beautiful gift to behold. This is a gift that is far larger than that of the most beautiful pianist in the world, or the fanciest painter in the world. The one that brings art in any form can never contribute to this point of helping people. For this is the largest, most beautiful, most abundant of gifts, the gift of love.

Love is the strongest gift, and in order to work with that spirit energy it takes an enormous amount of focus and love for you to help them after they expire from this earth sphere to move forward to that space of light to allow that light for the ones moving forward to see. Meaning you are a gifted, loving healer for those who are in that space, that critical space of moving from physical to the spiritual realm. Do you understand?

∞ *The Spirit's Journey* ∞

Rhonda: Yes

Laura Lyn: We would like you to devote your life to this cause; to this action, for this was what was written in your records. It was written that you would be one of the light workers of the world.

You may call them light workers, or earth angels, or healers but your critical point is to help those that are transferring from the physical to the spiritual realm. And we are pleased to work with you and will continue to help you to be able to distinguish the voice, the story, so that you can help them find their inner light and connect them to their grandmothers and grandfathers.

We are pleased to work with you and to speak with you about this critical energy that you bring to the world. Thank you.

Saving Lives through Sacrifice

Rhonda: Thank you. What negative energies may be left unresolved from past lifetimes that have created challenges for me in this lifetime that I need to work through for my spiritual and physical growth?

Laura Lyn: We would not refer to these as negative energies per say however, there is critical cellular tissue that is in your special energy internally that is inhibiting your movement forward. The release, while it may not be simple, is necessary and understanding where this came from in history will be helpful for you to release.

We will ask you to journal once you hear the story so that you can release through automatic writing. Simply write and allow it to flow through and the pain will be resolved accordingly. We are going to bring you back.

We understand that there was trauma from World War 1 that has brought you to a point of what they refer to as shell shock and now they refer to as post-traumatic stress syndrome. We are here to explain that you had been mortally wounded to the point where the pain was intolerable, unimaginable even, for you laid and suffered for three days unnoticed. You were lost and you died alone and this brought great pain.

And we are here to allow your knowledge that what came forward in the past is that you were able to save seven men's lives through your sacrifice but you did not have this knowledge. You had no knowledge of this. You could not have had knowledge. But it is critical for you to understand that you did save these seven lives and because of this hundreds of children were born into this world through the grandchildren.

And because of this, two scientists were born that helped in critical matters with making this planet a more green space because they have discovered ways to utilize energies in a way that is helpful to mankind. And so because of your sacrifice you did help change the world and this is important for you to understand.

So we request you to bring forward your words, your penmanship about the hurt, the pain, being wounded and alone and being released into the earth without notice for three days and the darkness that you took in from being lost. It took you some time to find that internal light, but in that space your soul retrieved, obtained the pain.

∞ The Spirit's Journey ∞

Now what happens in this sphere, in this magnitude, of your story now on this earth and journey is that that pain is still within the mass of that cell. And with that you may have fear of moving forward, fear of success, fear of helping, and fear of devotion. However these are your gifts and therefore there is the complication. Does this clear up matters for you?

Rhonda: It sure helps. Thank you.

Laura Lyn: Thank you Rhonda. We understand that this is painful knowledge however we do believe it's time for your understanding of this so you may release and move forward.

Rhonda: Is there anything of importance or helpful knowledge for me that I should still know that I have not asked you yet about?

Laura Lyn: We are understanding that you had many influences through Egypt. You had many influences through the pyramids. There was a time that you helped build the pyramids and you were very proud.

The square, the triangle these shapes were critical in your mathematic skills. Geometric energy is extremely powerful and you have brought forward much knowledge in the past. Understand that the shapes, the crystals, they hold energy for you from the past magical space.

When you hold a crystal you are holding the magic from beyond. You are bringing that magic back. You will always behold this magic and hold this magic. Therefore, by utilizing the energy of a crystal in your hand when you are helping people move forward, allow that energy to hold that circuitry, the energy that will help them align to that light.

Hold the crystal in your hand understanding that is the light they can see within, this is the true light. The Christ Light energy that is within the soul, within the heart, this is the truth that they are seeking to help them move forward. We are speaking of love, the light of love within, do you understand?

Rhonda: Yes. Would any of the experiences that I have had or, I'm trying to think of how to say it, are creating problems with me? Where I self-sabotage? When I'm trying to heal and I find myself moving forward then I force myself to draw back?

Laura Lyn: Again we see this as an issue from the past trauma that you faced and focused on in World War I and we are hopeful that you will be able to release this. We are grateful that you will be able to bring forward this release; for this will help you heal and bring you in a new direction that you will see the triumphant predestined plan of helping people heal and find this internal light; for this is an important ministry and we do foresee you utilizing this fully.

We do suggest if the writing is not sufficient to release this trauma a hypnotic trance session may be very beneficial to help release. For there you will be in a trance session living the moment and being able to release, erase, and forgive. However, we suggest that you work through writing to begin for you are ready to release this trauma.

Rhonda: Are there any other accomplishments or directions that you would feel that I need to accomplish or focus on?

Laura Lyn: We are hopeful that you understand the divine connection that you have with crystals. You have the capacity to be a strong healer through the crystals. The magnetic pole through your system aligns precisely with certain crystals that will help you bring forward prayerful healing and this can be for yourself, for a family member, a friend or a person you may be working with in the future as a client.

The critical energy that will be laying through the crystal in your hands will help bring forward passionate healing to your friend or to yourself or both because of your strong love and connection to spirit.

Healing from Within

Rhonda: What life lessons should I be learning?

Laura Lyn: Every relationship that you have been involved with has been healing and deep learning. You re-frequent many people from the past and you have done this cyclically through many life spans.

You are attempting to heal your past pain and trauma through other essence in people. However, the true trauma was within your own self and therefore the healing must come from within. And while you feel lonely or perhaps you feel challenged or controlled in a space of critical or criticized energy.

The truth is Rhonda the healing must come from within and move forward to a place of freedom. Allowing your heart to soar and rekindle with yourself. An individual cell within that aligns with that God consciousness energy and so full and abundant of love that you will be able to move forward and transform to a person that is completely understanding of your own beauty and light.

When that light shines through, you will attract the other that has the light. We understand that there are many decisions to be made and we understand that pain and trauma follows this. But we also see a new light for you in the future that will strongly transform your world as you know it and this we are excited for. Do you understand?

Rhonda: Yes.

Laura Lyn: We are grateful that this question was brought forward Rhonda. In this we see your strength. We understand the courage it took to ask this question, and we are here to help you. We will walk by your side as these critical decisions are made and as you grow. Learn and shine. We will be here to witness the celebration and for that we are very grateful. Thank you Rhonda.

Rhonda: Thank you.

Dale: Is there anything else you would like to say this evening?

Laura Lyn: Yes, my name is Edgar and I am here to help you. You have several allergies that are causing you intestinal upset. We are here to bring forward the following information to help you. Please remedy this and you will feel a drastic change internally.

You have a dairy allergy and a wheat allergy. They may refer to this as wheat sensitivity and an intolerance to

∞ *The Spirit's Journey* ∞

lactose. Understand that the cultures in live yogurt, the live cultures in yogurt are suitable for that is lactic acid and that will be beneficial for your internal body for repair.

Acidophilus and probiotics would be potent healers for you. As you release the toxins from your past trauma of life we are asking you to ingest live enzymes. The enzymes you can purchase at a food store that will be natural beneficial for you. The enzymes will help your body repair the cellular pathway where the trauma has brought forward much inflammation.

As you release this inflammation you will be releasing reserves of weight. You will feel yourself shed and as you shed, the emotional pain will be releasing. The process may take 6 months to a year but understand that this is energy that has been trapped for many years. So you will be releasing this rapidly.

We ask that you benefit your body by taking a multi-vitamin daily along with the enzymes, the probiotics for restoration and restoring balance within the flora system. The friendly bacteria will inhibit any fibroid growth that may take place or try to intrude while you are releasing the toxic energy from the past. Please understand that this information is for you to heal mind, body and soul. Thank you.

Rhonda: Thank you.

Dale: Do you have anything else to say this evening?

Laura Lyn: We are most grateful for this conversation, Thank you.

∞ Realm to Realm ∞

Dale: Thank you, we are very grateful for all of the messages this evening. And if you are done I would like to ask that you gently help Laura back to us and if it's possible give her a little energy boost on her way back. And again thank you.

---

[1] *This was a private session for our friend Rhonda.*

[2] Red Fox – Cherokee Spirit Guide

∞ Realm to Realm ∞
8-9-2011
Lumerians, Uriel
∞

Laura Lyn: We are grateful for your assistance and your light as we bring forward channeled messages through my sleep. We are asking for the ray of protection with Archangel Michael to encircle every one of us - to hold us during this time so we can be a clear channel for your knowledge and insight. I am asking for this ray of protection so only the highest greatest good, highest greatest light, and highest greatest sources come forward with their knowledge to share with the universe.

As we move forward we are so grateful for the energy and light. We are asking for your ray of protection to hold us for this half hour session where we will be seeking information for Trish, for her knowledge and pathway for the greater good. Thank you.

Lumerians – Collision of Knowledge

Dale: Who is with us this evening?

Laura Lyn: We are the Lumerians. We come forward with the knowledge of the seventh world of the seventh sphere. We are here to direct great light - great knowledge - for there are more spectacular forces that are working their way through, who will make an eventual collision of knowledge, of forthright energy, of truth.

We are here to bring this spectacular news. A new way of thought is among us. The new light, the new truth will

∞ *The Spirit's Journey* ∞

ignite through the frequency of vibration and thought patterns.

This ignition point and process, which we speak of, will bring a great balance and universal harmony upon this kingdom. This rapid energy of the spheres merging, the existence, dimensions, coming together.

There will be familiar energies among the Earth. There will be friends, truth seekers, messengers, guides, and angels alike. There will be nature spirits, sprites. There will be many other sorted energies of lower and higher vibration emerging.

The truth is that ascension is happening rapidly. We are grateful for your truth seeking and we will be here present and in the future to help you discern the truth.

Trish: How can we prepare for the shift?

Fear not for there is a true kingdom within your heart, within your personal spirit, your individual spirit. This is that consciousness of the Great Creator. Repeat I am, and understand that the God consciousness is within the cellular wall. The cellular energy is that great consciousness of light.

If you understand that you are truly part of this great energy, you will not lose your way. Light will always be eternally bright as long as you believe and are aware of that presence and are courageous to step through that veil of knowledge.

Trish: What happens when one passes and rejects that they have passed?

They may have a long darkness where they will have a space of true individual intent of fear. They may be in the abyss until they are ready to make the choice and decision that they are willing to see the true light that shines within their self.

They will eventually break free when they are ready to abandon the consequence of their own karmic addiction and direction: their karmic untruth. The truth is that life always sustains where light filters, meaning that we filter the great energy through our mirrored image of our consciousness of God.

Many will receive their new soul source, their light, their spirited self. They can help the consciousness of those who are in the abyss; those are on a sacred pathway, those are sacred pathway workers also. It is not necessary to stay on this Earth plane in order for soul survival.

Understand that we all have our own paths. Many leave this sphere to absorb into the great consciousness of light and love. Those warriors will find they will no longer have need to come back to reestablish or experience. There are many levels that the warriors, seekers, and light workers will emanate towards and be upon.

There are people among us, here on this earth plane that are from the great source, the cosmos and the direction from the sacred beginnings of creation.

Trish: How can people understand that they will be ok?

While their physical bodies do not understand, their physical minds, their higher selves certainly do resonate with their counsel. Every person here on this Earth plane is offered a sacred counsel which consists of assorted guides, messengers, angels, and beings of light.

There are those here who choose not to listen to their counsel. That is their choice. We are always granted choice. All humans are granted choice for the soul pattern and plan. Therefore they will have the opportunity to hear the great message, the great truth through their soul source – their higher knowledge. However, if they choose not to hear, and are grounded to the point of no return, they may lose their life and sink into the abyss state. They will still find the opportunity to turn around and regain truth through searching and eventually acknowledging the great truth of light where they will be released.

We Inhabit Many Dimensions

Will they do this in spirit? Or will they have the opportunity to manifest in a body?

They will have both opportunities. They will certainly have the opportunity before their death state. However, if they are into the spirit world, they will have the necessary opportunities in that place.

We inhabit many dimensions within this space in which you are sitting now dear child. Many directions, many levels are circling at this very moment. The space never stands still. It is in constant movement. Stagnation would kill all who inhabit that space. Therefore it is very necessary to be in this place of harmony and peace in each realm accordingly. And this is what we are establishing.

The great counsels have come forward to help realign the cosmos. While the axis has been moved on the Earth, many levels have been disturbed on the ethereal level. Therefore reestablishment is very necessary.

Universal Life Force

Are extraterrestrials here to help us?

Laura Lyn: We are understanding your question and what you speak of as extraterrestrials is simply universal life force that is coming through the cosmos on many dimensions. There will be many factors and presenters in many skins and many beliefs that will come forward for this reunion of life force.

The manipulated energy of radiation is causing havoc on the great mother. This will take time to cleanse and regenerate. There will be knowledge makers, seekers, and directors coming forth to cleanse this populated and polluted area so the Earth sphere can regenerate accordingly in expedited time factor.

The momentum is forming a new direction. We are here gathering the knowledge and seekers and the ones hungry for the great truth. To bring forward the direction that light will always win. The truth of love is always grand and there is the pivotal direction for life.

Dale: What can tell Trish her about her life path?

We are very dedicated Trish to your light, for we understand you have always been a seeker of truth and knowledge. You are one of the seekers and messengers that are here upon the Earth. We appreciate that you have pure intent to bring forward this knowledge.

∞ *The Spirit's Journey* ∞

Peace comes from all four directions. Look at the four directions and appreciate the land, the promise, bring forward the truth through your loyal heart. Love unconditionally. True harmony exists through the presence of the heart, the heart to share love, to guide, to bring forward and touch on another human existence.

We will hold the true light forward. We will always bring our energy of truth. We will open our doors so that others can balance through this great energy and admiration of light. We thank you for this time we have to share and will need to move forward. Thank you.

There is another messenger present.

Bring Light to this world

Trish: Who is the messenger?

We have Uriel, the great light and seeker of the angelic essence of the third sphere. This messenger is here to bring forward a message for Trish.

Understand that your insight is correct and rapidly opening. We love you dear child and have always been with you. We have brought you forward and directed you to people who are here to help. They are here to help you to understand your own wisdom.

We are here to guide you and hold your hand through this process. You will be brought forward through your light and your insight to a place that will be empowered. You will help open the knowledge of many.

Understand that you made a decision to bring light to this world in a selfless manner that was helpful and will bring great light. We love you unconditionally and will continue to sit and walk next you, our sister. We are finished. Thank you.

Dale: Thank you. We honor all messages you brought today. I would like to ask Laura's guides and angels that are working with her now to gently bring her back to us now to this place. And once again thank you.

∞ The Spirit's Journey ∞

∞ Realm to Realm ∞
8-14-2011
Ramiel, Sariel, Raziel, Rudolf Steiner
∞

It Began with Vibration

Laura Lyn: (humming)

Dale: is Laura ready to speak?

Laura Lyn: (humming)

Dale: Who's with us this evening?

Laura Lyn: Harmony and music is the breath of angels and the breath of the enlightened ones. You can greet thy lord through music. The passages, tones, and notes, offer inspiration, truth, and guidance. They are the Angel's words and the messenger's thoughts for they come through to people through a channeled way.

Understand that music is the passageway to spirit. Toning[1] is a powerful source to clear and release chaos. We call these points, these passages into the internal energies of your cellular system the chakras[2], for they touch the physical and ethereal.

Understanding the Sanskrit[3] language understood the right spin. The circumference of the circle taps into that inner being and the toning, the music vibration, is a forceful powerful way to cleanse the internal spirit.

And we are here to bring you the knowledge in the following tones to help each and every one cleanse and purify; allowing your breath to be the carrier resonating the tone in. Breathing in, allowing the tone to resonate within the chakras.

You will feel a clearing point and your adrenals will detoxify accordingly. As we prepare our voice there will be variances and tones that will sound hollow, flat. The healing vibration through the following tones, while audibly sounding uncomfortable, will bring a source of deep cleansing.

Laura sings various tones[4]

She continued to hum these tones for about 2 minutes.

What is Your Tone?

Laura Lyn: The sound of OM is a sound of AH, The sound of I, the sound within. This is the space of God. There are many debates out there, out in this consciousness on this earth, about gods, goddesses, about where it all began. The truth is it began with vibration. A consciousness that accidently rubbed upon the other, the friction of that consciousness, understanding of similar familiar energy.

The friction created a great sound, a great tone. This energy of what you call God sounded like OM which is the beginning. Through that particle exchange, other consciousness divided and some sounded like "OM" and others like (lower) "OM". Realize the feminine and the masculine sound, the powerful and the encompassing, and there you have the gods and the goddesses. But it all sounded and all formed, it all felt, it all was a vibration.

Your voice is a powerful vehicle. Yet those that do not have a voice that cannot speak carry a powerful vehicle through their consciousness, the thought. Allow yourself the memory of the first song you heard, the songs from the past that you enjoyed, for most likely they were very simple tones.

The reasons they were powerful was it brought you back to that god consciousness and your childhood memory. Your thoughts when you were a child where you remembered the OM, the vibration from the womb, the vibration from the universe.

Every petal on a flower vibrates with their own frequency. Every leaf on a tree has its own voice. Every animal has its own tone. What is your tone? Allow it to vibrate through your system and you're healing thyself.

You are here to remember the awesome power of the minute vibration for that recognition was contagiously aligned with love. It felt good to be recognized, to be familiar, and that transpired into multiplying.

Every angel carries its tone, its voice, its color. Aligning with these colors and frequencies, you are aligning with light, pure essence of light. The importance of toning, of bringing out the music, this is life changing. This will realign the human consciousness bringing people together as one.

This is our message tonight. Bring the music. Bring the tones and you are bringing the power of all. Thank you.

Dale: Thank you. Could you tell us who was speaking?

Laura Lyn: Yes. We have three angels that are speaking, the legion of Ramiel[5], who focuses on love and music.

Sariel who focuses on unity. And Raziel,[6] the one who always focuses on great energies of delight.

Aligning with Light

Dale: Do you have more messages you would like to share with us?

Laura Lyn: We understand that you are hearing the truth. We are understanding that you are hearing the new steps toward movement in this universe. Our boldness, our step forward on earth is indicated. For the inhabitants of this earth plane are bringing havoc and chaos; however, there are those who are also bringing peace and light.

The fear mongers, the ones who are bringing the darkness and consciously aligning with darkness through their possession and over consideration, even obsessive quality, this is attracting the darkness in a significant manner. This is attracted through media, exploitation, and antiquated thoughts. There has been an imbalance in the system. When the imbalance happens the great greed will win.

The highest beings of light are mistakenly thought of as Angels however, this is incorrect. The highest beings of light in truth are the ancestors that started in the beginning here on earth. They are those who have been here and witnessed the world throughout the stages, throughout its beginnings. They are here to help save this precious resource. They are here to bring battle upon the ego. They are here to bring battle upon the darkness that aligns with the culture of death and destruction.

While this super spiritual war is upon us, we are aligning with light seekers, and make no mistake that the darkness is aligning with those who are full of fear and dread. Those who want to bring havoc and violence, those who want to fight.

While it is necessary to prepare and defend by aligning with the light, it is much higher to make yourself invisible in time of war; to utilize the magic within, to be a sorceress of this light. We will grant permission and teach if this is what you are searching for. There have been many lessons that have been taught and there are many more if one seeks.

We promise you, to be by your every step. We promise to align as long as you ask. The elders, the wisdom keepers will be in the pathway. You will not perish but have an everlasting life. All is well, all is safe. Your ancestors are safe. Your descendants are safe. And while everyone has their individual path and choice, we are aligning with the highest good frequency. For who you are and where you belong is that of light.

Thank you very much. We bring blessings, healings and peace.

Dale: Thank You. Do you have more to say?

Three Feathers

Laura Lyn: We ask that each one in this room find their three feathers. Three feathers will be presented for they will bring you prosperity, healing and inspiration. They are a gift from the indigenous ones. The feathers will present themselves in the next three days. It is up to you to walk and look. You will find them. The feathers we ask that you keep for they will also bear great protection.[7]

The Spirit's Journey

We are all with you

Dale: how can we shield ourselves from darkness?

You are learning are you not? Keep moving forward with this. It takes diligence and lack of pride. Meaning a willingness to understand that strength comes from asking and courage is received. And Ben will be able to further teach you. It is now time for you to ask Ben for the knowledge of shielding.

Do you understand Dale? Ben can understand also? This can be a beautiful lesson to teach those who are searching for a higher blessing and lesson of truth. Dale is learning that the shielding must take place every morning. He is understanding that by placing that shield deliberately around the auratic field you are deflecting unwanted warriors. You are deflecting vile lies. You are deflecting chaotic memories that will distract from your truth.

There are many methods; however, the truth bears and the practice, a commitment, of this being habitual and before long it will be a matter of waking up and your shields are automatic. Is this not true Ben?

Ben: Yes it's totally true.

Laura Lyn: We would like you to teach Dale and we thank you.

Ben: You are very welcome.

Laura Lyn: Laura needs to fully awaken again. And we bless your evening and your day tomorrow. The feathers come from our friends. We are all with you in your waking days and your dream world sleep. We thank you.

[1] Toning – Laura describes the details of Angelic toning in her book *Healing with the Angel Rays*.

[2] Chakras – You can find a free Chakra Attunement online at www.angelreader.net.

[3] Sanskrit - is a historical Indo-Aryan language and the primary liturgical language of Hinduism, Jainism and Buddhism. Today, it is listed as one of the 22 scheduled languages of India and is an official language of the state of Uttarakhand. In western classical linguistics, Sanskrit occupies a pre-eminent position along with Greek and Latin in Indo-European studies.

[4] Watch angelreader.net for a CD containing these tones.

[5] Archangel Ramiel - is the angel of hope, and he is credited with two tasks: he is responsible for divine visions, and he guides the souls of the faithful into Heaven.

[6] Archangel Raziel – Inspires us to accept the mysteries in life. Name means God is my pleasure.

[7] Three feathers – When Laura woke up, she found a yellow feather at her feet. All of us found our three feathers within the three days.

∞ *The Spirit's Journey* ∞

∞ Realm to Realm ∞
8-16-2011
Light Beings
∞

This is session two with Trish.

Laura Lyn: We are gathering information for Trish. She is moving forward and getting information that will help in universal global ways. We are asking for your clarifications from the light beings that were with us last week. We are asking for them to step forward to be here for Trish's questions and I ask to go to a place of sleep.

Laura Lyn: I am feeling them all around me. You can start with the questions. They are here ready and I will go to sleep soon.

Light will Set You Free

Dale: Who is with us today?

Laura Lyn: We are here, there are many, we are light beings, here to focus our energy and our insight so that our distinctive energy can be known to the world. We are back. We have been here in ancient times gone by. We have learned much through our time here on Earth. We were here in peace. We were here to bring forward information. We gathered information from others in the past. We learned by their mistakes.

What we are bringing forward is that the light will set you free. This is and always has been the truth. This is what Jesus brought forward. He knew that this would be coming, and he was offering guidance through all, through God conscious energy that the light will set you free.

∞ *The Spirit's Journey* ∞

What we speak of is truth. The rapture[1] is truly a time when mortal men will see that their inner light that was created from that Great Spirit, great conscious energy, is truly of light. This sets them free and apart from evil. At that moment the shackles are removed and the spirit will be allowed to lift off to find their freedom to the everlasting light.

We would like to see the people follow the consciousness of light. For this is where truth lies; where truth is. There have been many manipulated ones out there who are receiving information from the dark sources. Unfortunately this source does not speak truth.

You see, the people of Earth, this planet, are the ones who either bringing greed or love, light or darkness. There are those helping the dark path and those helping the light path.

Different Planets?

Trish: Will there be an event that will help people understand that the angels are here to help us?

There will be many who see the angels. There are many who see the frequencies of light now. As the shift is moving forward they will see the magnificent colors and they will hear the tones. They will be part of this process. And they will understand from their consciousness, higher self, that indeed the angels are here to help them.

Trish: Are there people here who have come from other planets?

There are many beings of light here, who are here from many different realms, not necessarily different planets.

∞ Realm to Realm ∞

However, some of the planets possibly inhabited are energies of the past. There are many that are of the spirit realm present who inhabit human beings who have knowledge and insight. They may be your seers. They may be your doctors or lawyers. They all have specialized talents and are here with a mighty light to bring forward knowledge that love is the light that shines on.

We have several energies through the Dominions[2], and the Lumerians[3], Sumerians[4], we have the Crones[5], which are the ones who work through the indigenous energies through the native lands. We have those that are here who brought help from the past that are the Atlanteans. There are also those through the biblical resources that are shining a light onto this station and world.

We ask that you wake Laura for her energy is looming. We ask you to please allow her to wake.

Dale: We thank you for the messages I would like to ask that the angels and guides gently bring her back to this place and we thank you for the messages.

---

[1] Rapture – define from this book – previous session refer to it
[2] Dominions – are presented as the hierarchy of celestial beings "Lordships". The Dominions regulate the duties of lower angels. It is only with extreme rarity that the angelic lords make themselves physically known to humans. They are also the angels who preside over nations.
[3] Lumerians – Lumeria is the name of a hypothetical "lost land" variously located in the Indian and Pacific Oceans. The concept's 19th

century origins lie in attempts to account for discontinuities in biogeography.

[4] Sumerians – The Sumerian civilization took form in the Uruk period (4th millennium BC), continuing into the Jemdat Nasr and Early Dynastic periods. It was conquered by the Semitic-speaking kings of the Akkadian Empire around 2,270 BC.

[5] Crones – Indigenous Ancient ones.

∞ Realm to Realm ∞

8-19-2011

Spirit owl, Rudolf Steiner, Jophiel, and Spotted Owl

∞

Life is Love, and Love is Life

Dale: Who's with us this evening?

Laura Lyn: We have many present; Spirit owl, Rudolf Steiner, Jophiel, and Spotted Owl.

Dale: What would you like to tell us this evening?

Laura Lyn: The great truth is, and has always been, a space of the internal experience. That experience which the human being touches with their everyday desire, and how they approach life through the choices and decisions of their daily ordeals, and how they walk their path.

While random, or through the chosen direction; meaning that desired outcomes come forth during your day by first planting your seed of the vision then taking the steps forward to achieve the outcome that is desired.

We speak of love often as the chosen truth, destiny. However, the experience that falls in a daily life and quest, the experience, the expression of inner art and inner dreams is the true manifestation of light.

For the word love does become hollow if not brought into action through the challenge of the feeling unconditionally, meaning, looking at a person as their whole expression and loving them for who they are fully. This is the great truth, the experience, of the life individual and coming to a compromise, a decision, of desiring the self or loving unconditionally, selflessly. In that space and in that place life is love, and love is life.

We truly believe this is the destiny of the future. This is the energy that will transform not only this sphere, but many other dimensions. We will soon be colliding, and when this great exchange happens, when the dimensions drift within, love will be the ultimate challenge and choice for all, the internal point of bliss. Thank you.

You are Light

Dale: Do you have anything you'd like to tell our friend Jill?

Laura Lyn: We are pleased you are here Jill. You have travelled the road with Laura and Dale on this venture and you have seen and heard many sources of light. Understand dear one that you are also a source of light.

Sadly you have hidden that pearl inside of a lonely heart. The truth is dear one, that you can open up this heart expression at any time by simply willing yourself and saying I am light, I am love, I am forgiven, I am whole, and I am at peace.

That pearl will shine with a beautiful luster. The shined energy will come out and attract those of the highest vibration. They will see your light and the tears will not drop to the capacity as they have been dropping over the last decade. They will dry and your heart will sing. Your heart is ready to open by simply believing, knowing, allowing the pearl to shine we love you dear one. Thank you.

Dale: Thank You.

Honor the Children and the Elder

Laura Lyn: we have one more message.

Honor the children. It is so important to honor the children. Choose your words wisely. Look within. Unconditional love is necessary for all. It is so wise to honor the elder, to bring them in when situations are chaotic concerning the child. Pray to the elders that they will visit, watch and protect.

Along with their energy comes a stable familiar presence. By bringing in their energy you are helping the child grow and become wise with their daily decisions and mannerisms where they will respect the elder. Their higher self will be aware of the elders' presence so it is wise to bring in the wise ones by invoking their energy forward. Thank you.

Dale: Thank you. Is it ok to wake Laura now?

Laura Lyn: Yes.

(Waking Laura)

∞ *The Spirit's Journey* ∞

∞ Realm to Realm ∞
8-23-2011
Edgar Cayce, Rudolph Steiner, and Spirit Owl
∞

This is session three with Trish.

Laura Lyn: Archangel Michael, we are asking for your protective ray to come forward and to encircle us, to protect us in this space, and to protect us on the way home, so the highest greatest good - highest greatest light can come forward. Thank you.

Dale: Is Laura ready to speak?

Laura Lyn: Yes she is.

Dale: Who is with us today?

Laura Lyn: Edgar Cayce, Rudolph Steiner, We also have Angelic Frequencies, and Spirit Owl.

Beings of Light are here

Trish: Are enlightened beings here on earth? Will there be an event to enable mainstream media to prove that they are here?

Laura Lyn: What we anticipate is those who are searching and then being enlightened by these pillars of light, these beacons that they will communicate and talk. They will share and express what is being told and brought forward, such as you.

The enlightened beings processes to be here are happening at an unprecedented state. This is happening particularly over the last three years. Enlightened beings are here in spirit form, and in human physical form. They are also here in protected form, meaning beings of light will speak to people who are actually a projection from other sources, other spaces.

Trish: Do the enlightened beings know who they are? Do they need to awaken to fulfill their life plan?

They are already awakened. Their soul level is awakened to their journey, their pathway. They will be reminded through their higher knowledge, higher self, of what their path intentions are on a conscious level. Awakening happens at your own destined time and space. We welcome the information that will be filtered through. Those who desire to search higher identities, higher truths, will stumble upon the information, but again it is not necessary to awaken all. It is not necessary to push.

Understand that their life destiny and plan is still being fulfilled here on earth. There are light energies and light angels and dark energies and dark angels on this earth. The light path that every individual is living is of their highest realm, highest light. Therefore, whether or not they have the knowledge within of who they are does not resonate with whether or not they are living their life path. They are living indeed their path in a manner their knowledge or insight of who they are or whether or not they are. Aware has no bearing on their ministry.

It is completely acceptable for every individual to move along their own path and you will find yourself in a space, eventually, bringing forward your great news and your great message through the higher learning, higher being, and higher light.

The ones who are supposed to get the information will in their own way. There are many seekers who are hungry for this information. And for those this will resonate. People will hear and understand the new message of love and light of truth harmony, of peace. This new message will help change the world as we know it.

Alien Beings?

Trish: Are there beings here from other planets?

Some beings absolutely were on different planets in the past, however, the inhabited space of the earth has been the subjective core for many years, many thousands of millennium. And therefore, the energies that are here come from this space, this earth.

Understand that the earth beings, the earth lights, that are here come from angelic frequencies that are many layers of God conscious energy. This is the energy of the great creator. The creator created this space, this time, this energy from a powerful source of energy that erupted.

The cosmos does deliver many frequent visitors that unite with us. However the core comes from this indigenous space, this space that was the beginnings of time. The information, that of the elders, comes from the core.

Many energies – people, spirits who are here are here to help enlighten, are here for this planet only. We are feeling that there is mass confusion on a secular group and people are being misled by the feeling that other planets that inhabit space of these higher beings.

The truth is that the energy was always here all around us on our core, on our space, on our time. The dimensions therefore are also here. We have space, the time, the energies, and there are other super cosmos that holds its own consciousness that will bleed through from time to time. There are seekers, there are watchers, and there are towers that come forward to bring energy and to borrow space and energy. There are those that are being projected, but they are not from what you refer to as planets, but rather they are from other realms of the space continuum.

Trish: Can we telepathically communicate with these beings?

Everybody has focused energy that helps them on their life path. It is simply a matter of meditation and learning the process. While everybody does not have the same frequency and ability to precisely receive messages, those who are searching certainly through the process of practice and aligning with the energies will perceive the information properly and in due time.

Dale: Is Laura becoming depleted?

Laura Lyn: We suggest that you wake her up.

Dale: we ask that Laura guides wake her and bring her back to this place gently and completely. Thank You.

∞ Realm to Realm ∞

9-18-2011

Rudolf Steiner, the Lumerians

∞

Dale: Who's with us this evening?

Laura Lyn: Rudolf Steiner

Dale: What would you like to say to us tonight?

Have Faith

Laura Lyn: Let me begin by expressing our deepest thanks and gratitude. We are here as a group to bring forward the following information. The sequence of events that has been offered is by no accident.

There will be a time in the not so far future the money will not spend in the same way and this will cause a catalyst of fear. The information that is being brought forward will help many feel and understand that indeed there is no reason to fear. For there will always be plenty through the resources that will follow.

The spirited helpers and guides will present themselves. Those who are here in this room are learning to tap into their source. They will carry you. They will lead you to where you can get bread and fresh water so despair not for you are learning the truth that your needs will always be supplied as long as you hold faith.

This is why indeed love is always the answer. For as long as you hold this deep gratitude to the conscious Great Spirit, the presence will always be at your shadow. The meek inherit this earth. The humble survive. The courageous ones, the ones that hold love will conquer all.

This is the true mercy. This is the true strength. The true warrior of today's time is through love, not blood. Understand that it takes a lot more strength to love than it does to hate. This is the true weapon of today's time. Hold it, bring it forward, and allow it to be your badge of honor. We will always be with you to help you. We bless you and thank you.

All has Purpose

Dale: Thank you. Is there anything you can tell us about the energies that have been coming through in our previous sessions?[1]

Laura Lyn: We understand your question. There is a purpose for every energy. There is a purpose for every encounter. And understand the messengers that were brought forward, while they were not in the same frequency of light as you were accustomed to, do have deep purpose.

Understand that we all came from individual truths and paths. There are those who are tapping into beings that are from other spaces and places across the galaxy. While their energy is certainly not dark, it is a different caliber of energy that is too dense for this planetary system at this active point.

The energy beings are being projected here to bring their story or to collect knowledge. They mean no harm. They are here for their existence and survival just as you are. They are interested in this planetary system to bring back information for their own, and to research the possibility of landing and being in this space for their existence in the future.

There are many truths and many lands. The existence of the truth that is being tapped into is not evil. However it does not carry the message that is resourceful for your passage and word. The world needs this work that you are bringing forward. Seekers and messengers are hungrily absorbing the information.

Hold the light on this and allow the ones that are expecting the exorbitant amount of time through a pressured sense. Allow them to slip through your fingers, for they are tapping into resources that are precious and few.

The message here of love and light has the utmost important stance. We will deliver this continually as long as you are open and have the energy to absorb this information. We are unable to infiltrate if the resources are taken. Therefore it is requested that you allow the messengers of love to come through as frequently as possible. Thank You.

Dale: Thank You. Ben has a question.

Contagious Energy

Ben: What can I do to put my ideas forth in a more positive manner?

Laura Lyn: While we did not hear a negative stance that you are speaking of, it is always important to bring information through your heart. This information would then be your truth. We find that when you or anyone enriched their self with positive aspect, positive light, that this contagious energy comes through. We invite you each day find your morning with gratitude. We appreciate your humble question and we assure you, we understood your questions and your comments. Your message today and last Sunday was meant for knowledge and not insult therefore we do not encourage any change. Just continue with your truth. Thank you.

Ben: Thank You

History is the Lesson

Dale: I'd like to ask Rudolf Steiner, what is it that's attacking me on a regular basis? Is it my thought choices? Is there something that I'm unaware of that's causing my struggles every now and then?

Laura Lyn: We are of the knowledge that your history has been very chaotic, traumatic, and painful. Therefore you look at history as insult. You look at history as an enemy. That could be the history of yourself, your wife, possibly your friends.

History, dear man, is not the enemy it is the lesson. Somehow we learn from what was damaged through us and to us. The damages that have been bestowed upon us are often karmic effects from a lifetime that was unchartered and unclosed.

When the lesson is learned and understood, and you become that source of light that we speak of, it is possible to release and we understand that you received the message today of how to release this.

Respect the oil[2]. It comes from your past. It comes from a place when you were in Africa and you hurt many women.

It comes from a space where you humiliated many people, when you hurt children. It is time now to release this for you have found mercy.

You have found yourself wanting to help those in jail for a reason. It is time now to understand that the one in prison has been you. You have locked yourself up from all the damage you have caused.

Release the remorse in the water. High John oil is a deep African root system that you have used in the past through the hoodoo, voodoo traditions. Allow that energy to surpass and this vile energy of jealousy and repression will expediently be released.

The pain that you received from the history will be eradicated. The suspicion you feel for others will be erased. The envy, the jealousy, all this pain will be eliminated in this one simple session and this bath. You will no longer live with this self-hatred. Do you understand?

Dale: I don't feel jealously or envy towards people so I don't understand.

Laura Lyn: Not towards people, with people.

Dale: I still don't understand.

Laura Lyn: When you are with your wife; when you were witnessing others from her past. The deep conscious level within is that of your past. Understand that the levels are deep within your subconscious. Do you understand?

Dale: Yes.

Laura Lyn: Thank you.

The Powerful Light

Dale: Do you have anything else you would like to say?

Laura Lyn: We sense fear. We sense doubt. We are here to assure everyone the light is very powerful. You will find this light so much more powerful than any darkness that has ever been upon you.

We are here to destroy the bitter energy, the bitter reality of what happened to millions of people who were persecuted for their religion (*throughout history*). Millions of people who are persecuted for their place in life the resources, and those who have died of genocide or ethnic cleansing.

The energies that will be brought forward will help cleanse the wrongs of man for thousands of years. This pain must dissipate so the wars will stop raging. The karmic effects, the clouds of this continuous confusion, must be released to see the love that is spoken of so often.

You see, with this muddied energy of hate flaming continuously in the atmosphere, it is literally and utterly impossible to align with that precious light, that foundation. This is true redemption. This is the true space of light. This is the true Christ consciousness coming back to the earth.

This cleansing must take place in order to see the face of Jesus, the face of god, the face of man, all three in this trinity of light, and the princess, the lady, and the mother, the sacred energy of the feminine path, continuous path of love through the means of the heart.

Dale: Thank you.

Laura Lyn: We thank you.

Message from the Lumerians

Laura Lyn: *Laura speaks in another language at 37 minutes into the session. She speaks for about a minute.*

Dale: Can you translate that?

Laura Lyn: We are here to announce that the beginning of the salvation is here as the prince of love. We will not allow the temptation of the darkness to bestow their wicked ways upon this sacred work and duty. We will be here to protect you we will be here to align with this work[3] that must take place.

We are here and will not allow you to be astray, for this important work will change the world as you know it. We will not allow you to go astray.

Dale: Can I ask who was speaking?

Laura Lyn: We are here as a mission. We are the **Lumerians** that you have heard from in the past. It is true we are here to help.

The Atlanteans are a sector that are infiltrating. The Atlanteans of the second sector are filled with greed and destroyed their land. They are the chaotic nuances have been infiltrating this world for thousands of years. These are the destroyed energies that you see time and time again with the genocide and the horrible slaughter of men and women and children.

Trust our word. We are here to help you find your strength. We are here to help you, protect you, as you do this important work. Thank you.

∞ *The Spirit's Journey* ∞

Dale: thank you. I'd like to ask that Laura's counsel angel guides help to bring her back to this place and we thank you for the messages.

---

[1] Energies from previous sessions – Refers to the Lumerians.

[2] High John Oil – (also called John the Conqueror Oil) is believed to aid in all accomplishments. Promotes mental abilities and clear thinking. This oil is considered to be excellent for overcoming obstacles.

[3] This work –This book and the mission of our center.

∞ Realm to Realm ∞

9-19-2011

Rudolf Steiner, Counsel

∞

Dale: Is Laura Ready to speak?

Laura Lyn: Yes.

Dale: Who's with us today?

Laura Lyn: Rudolf Steiner is here.

Dale: What do you have to say to us today?

Laura Lyn: I request that you ask direct questions please Dale.

Fighting to Become Anew

Dale: I know I got some advice about using oils. What else can I do to work past this struggle of being happy, then crashing into despair? It's gotten much better and less frequent. Is this something that I can get past?

Laura Lyn: You will. It is a process. The purpose of the oil is to take you back to a time when you have used deep magic. (see previous session) You would put the oil together yourself. At this point you were considered a voodoo priest. Just as there are people of all sorts, there are priesthoods of all sorts.

Your life took a direction of intent to harm and this hurt many. The oil will help reverse and release all karmic ties. It will help you release the chaos and the sadness on a very deep level.

∞ The Spirit's Journey ∞

You will see the abrasions in your skin start to clear after this process. You are holding on to a root level of pain. And this is the skin eruptions. The psoriasis comes forward through an overstated guilt system. You are now fighting to become anew.

You find yourself feeling bad because in your perceived notion you are falling short. The truth is you are exactly where you should be regarding the potential of your highest field you have released. You have done beautiful work and we are honored to work with you.

Understand that this feeling of inadequacy came to you from a conditioned response from your past. This place of discomfort was conditioned but you have an opportunity to break out now. This will bring you new opportunities in the future, where there will be no more annoyance and discomfort within the groups

It is necessary to bypass and rise above and find the comfort level. For you have work to do, and it will be important to use your voice; so it is necessary to chime in the conversation accordingly. We anticipate that once you start to utilize your voice, you will find that you are actually enjoying the experience that you are presently in.

Your wife and friends care about you and love you. They accept you unconditionally. They love you more than you love yourself at the present moment. It is time to receive love within total acceptance and release the burden of the past; this is what we are offering.

You are at a true space where you can jump that plank. Release the old and receive the new. It is a beautiful space to be in, and we will witness the miracles of this true release.

Dale: Thank you. I am also honored to work with you. This is an amazing experience. Even with the low times I experience, I'm gaining ground.

The Threshold of Death

Dale: Are there times within this life that we kind of "Die"? There have been times that I felt I was there.

Laura Lyn: You have stated and you have witnessed the passing of time and transcendence through the death state. You are correct.

Dale: Could you tell me about your teaching that describes meeting your doppelganger?[1]

Laura Lyn: The doppelganger as I perceived it when I was on this earth plane is quite different than the actual stated being presentation. What I'd like to refer to is a quick spirit[2]. It is a spirit that jumps in and mirrors your effect. It mirrors your personality and it moves along with this mirrored outcome as an act. It affords the spirit a body and an image so they can feel life for interval amounts of time. The bodied spirit jumps in and allows this mirrored image system to be their own for a short amount of time. You have indeed been replicated and you have indeed *folked* up.[3]

Dale: Is the quick spirit something we can experience during times of either sadness or joy?

Laura Lyn: correct

Dale: Does this "quick spirit" influence us?

Laura Lyn: It only mirrors us. It has no reflection or influence on us as individuals

Dale: So the "quick spirit" has no influence on an individual. What is it that seems to be attacking me?

Laura Lyn: These are issues from your past, frequencies of pain or insult. Do you understand?

Dale: The thought patterns I am working on seem like subconscious addictions. I have been thinking that breaking the addiction cycle can't be forced but must come from understanding.

Laura Lyn: We see addiction as a cruelty to self. We see it as a repetitious behavior that is rooting inside a place of perceived weakness. Addiction carries a historical root, a place of pleasure in the past in order to obtain self-satisfaction. It is the root of selfishness.

When one releases this circular reaction, they are eliminating the past root system of this activity. This, my friend, is complete freedom. Then you are able to truly know and feel love on the selfless attained state.

Acceptance is the main feature of release; believing in the spirit and the strengths thereof, and forgiveness. Releasing through forgiveness; you are then cleansed and all karmic effects dissipate.

Helping Yourself to Help Others

Dale: Thank You. Do you have anything else that you'd like to say?

Laura Lyn: We see your strength. We see how hard you are working through the conditioned patterns.[4] You are where you are because of the directions of your past. This has corresponded to our truth of balance and order; the destiny of love rising above.

We will be with you through this process. We promise not to desert you. You have had many rich experiences that most could only dream of in this spiritual quest. This is a rich resource and opportunity for you. And while you rise above, it is a rich and rewarding experience for us, for we are connected to this ascension as well.

We will both rise above and for this we are very grateful.

Dale: Thank you I'm very grateful too. I feel the presence of all of you throughout the day and I speak with you all. In the back of my mind I sometimes wonder if you're there but most of the time I know you're there. I trust that and I really do have a lot of gratitude for that.

Laura Lyn: We have a very deliberate strong counsel here. There is the understanding that deep magic will persist. You family and friends have known deep trauma, sadness and fear. Everyone has also learned and known deep joy, passion, and love. Love is at the center.

We find it sad that we do not feel you understand the depth of the love that they have for you and the admiration they have for you.

Every member sees you as a wise soul and is looking for your appreciation and your admiration for them.

We thank you.

Dale: Thank you for putting it that way because this work gets me wrapped up in working on self-growth and

change. That will give me a good way to look at everything.

Soul Groups – Our Counsel

Dale: You're all my counsel as you are Laura's counsel?

Laura Lyn: That is correct. This is a soul group. We have all known each other. We are all here together again. The mysteries will start unraveling and the light will shine a new understanding when you are ready. But for now just understand that we have all known each other.

Dale: Should I wake Laura is she becoming tired?

Laura Lyn: We feel it would be wise to let her come back to this space.

Dale: I'd like to thank all of you and I'll be talking to often.

Laura Lyn: You're welcome our dear friend.

Dale: Thank you, my dear friends.

Be Kind to Yourself

Laura Lyn: We have one last message. Please be kind to yourself. When you're feeling the depths of despair, bring yourself back to a space of helping others heal. They have not even tapped into their despair yet because they are quite in the field of the vibration area that does not support the memory.

Others will come to the depths of their depression and they will need your understanding and kindness. Understand that this is a large order but we know that you are able to help for you have experienced it to the depths. Do you understand?

Dale: Yes. Thank you for being here.

Laura Lyn: You're welcome.

(waking Laura)

---

[1] Meeting your doppelganger - This refers to a time during spiritual development that puts one outside oneself. Then one is able to regard oneself without condition. The beginning of realizing unconditional love.

[2] Quick Spirit - This is a mirroring type of "spirit fusion" that does not influence the host. This type of possession could be an experience that aids in the expansion of the "possessing" spirit.

[3] Folked up - Breaking free of conditioned routine patterns at the soul level. This could also be described as an evolvement of an individual and/or group "soul pattern".

[4] Conditioned Patterns -Release from "prison", begs to be put back in. The cage became "home"

∞ *The Spirit's Journey* ∞

… *Realm to Realm* ∞

11-7-2011

Rudolf Steiner
∞

Laura Lyn: Dale, I'm getting a message. I'm not asleep but I'm strongly hearing him speak. He's humbled and proud at the same time because he's been working with you individually and very strongly through the year, and you have conquered him.

Dale: What does that mean?

Laura Lyn: That means that Yurishah, is a daemon[1] who has been intruding on the process and progress. You fought through and conquered so that this being can no longer insult you by disallowing your talent to shine. Do you understand?

Dale: Is that why I've felt better this past week?

Laura Lyn: Absolutely. Rudolf Steiner is speaking. You are in a place now where you will be more free to invent. You will be more free to create. Does this resonate?

Dale: Yes. Thank you.

Protection – Cleansing and Sealing your space

Dale: Can you give us any ideas on how we can keep other negative things that are fighting our progress at bay?

Laura Lyn: We have provided information to you about High John oil. This has been helping clean the auratic field on the first, second, and third chakra system. This will continue to help you as long as you continue the oil presence. Please continue the baths.

The oils can be used at any time. It is to be used over all doorways and seals throughout the house. There is a beautiful group here at this present moment that can help complete the task of the cleansing of the home by the love and energy pouring through and blessing all seals with the oil. It may be necessary to do this quarterly and through the center monthly, for seals do weaken.

If you realize there are darkened energies, it is imperative to act swiftly by utilizing Archangel Michael's energy. It is also helpful to work with Chamuel[2]. Bring her energy forward through her feminine process and essence for the vibration of her frequency is not inviting to the darkened space. Do you understand?

Dale: Yes. Thank you.

Laura Lyn: Your space and time is in a perfected place to reveal the truth of love and simplicity; the truth of connection and focus; the heightened awareness that all is connected through love. Bring forth the compassion and the strength, release the fear.

Please bring our message forward of love and light. We would like to hear the acceptance for our counsel is here with you in this circle. We would like to have meetings with you both on the spiritual level through these talks and your interpersonal physical meetings we will always be by your side do you understand?

Everyone: Yes

Please bring forward the true message of love, the true message of joy and laughter, and be in awe that we are one together.

The Butterfly effect

Dale: I'll just ask one more. I wanted to know if you wanted to clarify your lecture *Reading to the Dead?*[3] Is there anything you would like to say about it?

Laura Lyn: We have always understood a certain lot about the three levels. However, it is understood at this moment that true death only happens when a certain lot is in the darkness doorway where there is no understanding of connection within their cell. Otherwise, the dead is not a complete accurate word for life always remains in the physical existence as you know it in this level and beyond. Does this resonate?

Dale: So it would be reading to other Realms?

Laura Lyn: Exactly. And that is why it is understood. Realm to Realm is dimension to dimension and galaxy to galaxy, space to space. The dead are on many levels and the fear of the dead brings that consciousness that some may call evil.

However, they are merely lost and it is impeccably disastrous for the conscious souls to be unconscious. So the works that you bring forward through the rescued points raises the vibration for a whole. Even on a minuscule level, the butterfly effect[4] remains. Do you understand?

Dale: Yes thank you. Should I be waking Laura?

∞ *The Spirit's Journey* ∞

Laura Lyn: We recommend so. Thank You.

Dale: It's been a pleasure hearing all your messages tonight. We thank you and honor you. I am asking that Laura's angels and guides gently wake her and bring her back to us. Thank You.

---

[1] Yurishah - is referred to as a daemon. In the Authorized Version of the New Testament, daemons are spoken of as spiritual beings (Matt. 8:16; 10:1; 12:43-45) at enmity with God, and as having a certain power over man (James 2:19; Rev. 16:14). They belong to the number of those angels that "kept not their first estate," "unclean spirits," "fallen angels" (Matt. 25:41; Rev. 12:7-9). They are the **"principalities and powers"** against which we must **"wrestle"** (Eph. 6:12).

[2] Chamuel - is an angel in Judeo-Christian mythology and angelology, and is often included in lists as being one of the seven archangels. The name means, "One who seeks God." Also known as an angel of Love.

[3] *Reading to the dead - I had been reading a lecture regarding how to help loved ones who have passed. It was from the 1920's and went into some excellent concepts about "spirit rescue". We received some new ways to look at the subject throughout this session and the next session on 11-21-11*

[4] Butterfly Effect - In chaos theory, the butterfly effect is the sensitive dependence on initial conditions; where a small change at one place in a nonlinear system can result in large differences to a later state.

∞ Realm to Realm ∞

11-21-2011

Edgar Cayce, Rudolf Steiner, Zadkiel
∞

A Sum of Opportunities and Experiences

Laura Lyn: Dale if you want to go ahead, I feel that they will come through

Dale: What happens when one does pass and leave the physical existence?

Laura Lyn: Unfortunately, there has been much confusion on this area for we have our own conclusions about death and life even as the spirit presence. The inner cell of life existence is simply a sum of the opportunities and experiences of a lifetime; therefore, the difficulty lies within the explanation of life and death.

Each cell, *each soul*, holds its own information which radiates upon the heaven sphere. Each cell holds its own journey just as each individual on the earth plane holds its own life plan and mission.

The Souls They Need Your Work

The complexities of explaining the spirit realm within the death experience is an enormous pursuit. We feel it would be better suited to share the excitement that the individual can bring upon when communicating with a spirit that needs help, what you refer to as spirit rescue is important.

The souls they need your work. They need your message, and they need your light, so they can indeed find their inspiration and move forward. There are three levels which you can work with and through at any time.

These three levels are indeed searching for the discovery of light. It is of the utmost importance that they find this inspiration so they can be freed to move upon this journey.

You are presented with this crossroad; they are presented with the opportunity to shine upon their discovery of truth. Truth is revealed at an enormous speed of light. Bring them to the understanding, the "dead", that they are indeed alive. Death is an illusion.

Communicate with them and they will rapidly hear the truth. Bring to them the truth of love and connection. They are buried with the illusion that they are separate from God, and truth is and always was that the connection is within the space of their self.[1]

With this truth comes upon a rapid understanding, and there they see their elders, ancestors, path, and their soul path community. And in that light shines the greatest happiness and this dear one is the joy that we bring forward. That is the reason for life. As this joy rises, the essence of the whole will rise.

This is the rebirth, the rapture of truth. Sing with this, be with us, and we will shine forward. This is the true light of love, the true light of consciousness.

Proper Diet for Strength

Dale: What can we do to protect ourselves while doing this work?

∞ Realm to Realm ∞

Laura Lyn: We have Edgar Cayce here. Dale, it is important that you understand that you heard the correct formula (St. John's Wort[2] and Ginkgo Biloba[3]) for your brain mechanism, synapses firing completely.[4]

We will continue to work with you to bring you information but the eating habits are causing ill effect and sludge throughout the system that is slowing down the processes. Do you understand that the food that you eat brings vital life and energy into the system? You are eating foods that are dead in nutrition value. This is causing the processes to slow and a certain vulnerability to come in.

We beg of you to at your earliest convenience to buy fruits and vegetables. And to start the process of the diet that has been brought forward. To clean the system and after you get to a manageable place where the fog is lifted to understand that the smoke is not necessary and your growth would be much more rapid once it is released.

We understand that this is difficult. However through a hypnotic statement that can be recorded and listened to nightly this new life style is not only attainable but simpler than you believe through the process. We anticipate this being an exciting adjustment for you both. Please hear our words. The diet must change and the smoke must be released for the true growth to be at the highest potential. Do you understand?

Dale: Yes. Thank you.

Dawning a New Day

Dale, with all the complications of your lifetime span, presence and experiences, you are dawning a new day where joy will be the deep answer and in this space you will never wonder why you are here. You will always understand with great joy that the answers are flowing, and the connections are at bay. We are having a reunion and we delight in this.

Jessica, your spirit and presence has always been sweet and loveable. You were and are a true spirit child. Your innocence is beautiful. We welcome you with great delight as we feel your renewed strength and love. We are excited for you.

Jessica: Thank You.

Laura Lyn: You are quite welcome.

The Reason for Existence

Becky you were always so humble and loveable and I find myself with tears now happy that your joy is coming to the surface the true joy, not the mask of your past laughter, but the true joy in your heart that you truly belong and are loved.

And Dale your wisdom is shining through. You are at a place in this deep contemplation that the simplicity is and will be revealed.

The truth is that the reason for existence is quite simple. The sphere, the spaces, where the beings of light, the messengers, the masters, and the elders lay, is right here and right now; within our sphere we all have communication and order; within that space we have all of the sum of all our experiences.

We are all individual yet complete at the same time. Please present this information through the simple truth of love and we will all ascend together. Thank You

Everyone: Thank You

Dale: We honor you and truly thank you for everything you have said tonight. I should wake Laura. It has been 40 minutes. (*Asking to wake Laura*)

Laura Lyn: We are quite illuminated at this moment and at peace. We thank all of you also.

Message from Zadkiel [5]

We are here to share a message of glory and light. Truth the great truth of love transcends all. The precious beings of love and the children of the world are here at this moment to bring forth a great truth and great glory of light!

This light shines upon the earth at this moment. This precious love, this love that is like a brilliant sphere from the greatest star, is here to bring forward the truth of the Christ light, the Christ consciousness, that consciousness that is here and now, that consciousness that he has brought forward that has transcended all races, all origins and all space. The wisdom of all the human race is here together in one great place, this place that is now known as one.

Oneness, that great space, is here and now. Do you see? Do you hear? Do you understand that the great place of oneness is actual truth for this is the space and time that communication can take place across the world; this is the place that was prophesized in the bible.

∞ *The Spirit's Journey* ∞

This is the wonderful time that the beautiful message is coming forward. But fear not for revelations was a misinterpretation. It is not the ending but a great beginning. A new truth, a new light, a new beginning, a journey that is taking place that is of the precious light of God.

Therefore dear children understand that our love, our light, our message is coming forward rapidly. The love from the angels, the bliss from the goddess, the sheer rapid strength of the gods, is coming forward on this world now and will take place, will take precedence, for there is a true journey of hope.

We see a new road that is written in the books that will bring forward the ancient truth of one. We are here. We are now. It is time.

This is the pursuit of the rapture. The rapture in its truth is to release the fear of bondage. There will be a great quake, there will be a great change in the economy, there will be a space and time here rapidly bringing forward a light.

But with that a great truth will follow. There is no reason to fear children. Your needs will be met as long as you understand that seek ye first the wisdom, the presence of God, and all shall come upon you.

You will not starve in the midst; you will be strengthened and nourished. We love you and we will always be with you by your side magically helping you. We bless you dear children

Dale: Thank You. Could you tell me who was speaking?

∞ Realm to Realm ∞

Laura Lyn: You know me as Zadkiel.

Dale: Would anyone else like to speak?

Laura Lyn: We will allow her to wake.

Dale: Thank you.

(waking Laura)

---

[1] Spirit Rescue – This is a very useful concept to use during spirit rescue: *Communicate with them and they will rapidly hear the truth. Bring to them the truth of love and connection. They are buried with the illusion that they are separate from God, and truth is and always was that the connection is within the space of their self.*

[2] St. John's Wort - is widely known as an herbal treatment for depression. In some countries, such as Germany, it is commonly prescribed for mild depression, especially in children and adolescents.

[3] Ginkgo Biloba - Ginkgo is mainly used as memory and concentration enhancer, and anti-vertigo agent.

[4] I had purchased these two supplements about three months before this session. They were sitting unused in my desk. After hearing this I began to use them on a regular basis and have experienced excellent results.

[5] Message from Zadkiel - *After I asked that Laura wake up, she began this message. She spoke much faster than usual and she was very loud, almost yelling.*

∞ *The Spirit's Journey* ∞

∞ Realm to Realm ∞

12-11-2011

Rudolf Steiner, Edgar Cayce, and Spotted Owl

∞

Aliens- Ancient Battles

Dale: We have questions about aliens. Is there any connection to the ancient civilizations from 12 to 14,000 years ago?

Laura Lyn: The name alien is erroneous. It brings in error because these are enlightened beings that are spoken of often through Laura and through others in this great world.

The enlightened beings from the past are enlightened by their wisdom that came from the ages thousands upon thousands of years ago.

There will be many discoveries on this great earth, this great planet, where civilizations will be uprooted from 15,000, 20,000 and even 30,000 years.

The ancient enlightened beings understood mathematics and how to harness energy upon these plots, ley lines, and grids. They understood how to harness the field of magnetic. They understood a precision line of cutting. They utilized this sacred memory of knowledge to cut away stone, to fragment, and to align the stones in certain patterns that replicated and brought forward a map, a beacon for these beings to launch, lift, and move from.

The beings readily moved back and forth upon the earth until a great fight conquered many of the beings upon civilizations and the races. Just as the history that was very recent shows you through ethnic cleansing, the race of the earth defeated many of the enlightened ones through ego. This is the true spiritual warfare. The lower vibrations conquered many of the enlightened ones, harnessed their energy, and killed their spirit.

So now you are left with higher beings and lower beings at a constant turmoil. You may feel this chaos as upheavals on the earth manifest; the great flood that was replicated here in the United States not so long ago. Many of the darkened energies fed on that turmoil. This energy will continue to defeat the weak, the vulnerable, the sick, and the poor. Consider the enlightened beings: the Angels, the Goddesses, the Gods, and the wisdom makers. These are your aliens. Do you understand?

Everyone: Thank you

The remaining part of this session has been edited (by request) in order to remove personal questions and answers.

∞ Realm to Realm ∞

1-5-2012

Rudolph Steiner, Edgar Cayce, and Raphael
∞

The New Home upon Earth

Dale: Who's with us tonight?

Laura Lyn: We have Rudolph Steiner, Edgar Cayce and Raphael

Dale: What would you like to tell us tonight?

Laura Lyn: There are many waiting to see this new dimension that is on the edge of revelation. This new dimension is on the edge of revealing the truth of light, the new truth of love, the new truth of strength.

What we are petitioning is a vibrant essence of devotion. This will be a new way, a new frontier for this world to speak and see. This will be a new companionship for brothers and sisters. This will be a place where faith and truth will succeed. There is a new anchor presenting itself and the knowledge that is transcending the earth is that which is forming from the heavens.

The new anchor is the enlightened ones, the beings of light, travelling and opening that space of true commitment, commencing love. We are certainly enchanted by the knowledge of this new space and time. We are recommending that you approach this new millennium energy with respect honor, and certain gratitude, for the gods and goddesses are forming the new home upon the new earth.

∞ The Spirit's Journey ∞

(*Specific personal information removed*)

Bring Your Light

Dale: Do you have anything else to tell us this evening?

Laura Lyn: We are rapidly moving towards this new world that was called upon. There is no mistake; every human being on this earth at this moment is here for a special purpose and reason. Many will hear their inner voices and some may not. Those who do move forward will have direction with their alignment situation, for those who are being taught a certain spirited direction of rescue. No souls will be lost as long as they do not fear. Fear is the mortal enemy. Therefore bring your light, bring your eyes to the light of love, and all shall be well.

—Asking to wake Laura

This was a personal session. I removed all personal references and only retained the introduction and ending statement.

∞ *Realm to Realm* ∞

2-5-2012

Mary, Children of the Sun

∞

Children of the Sun

Dale: Is Laura ready to speak?

Laura Lyn: Yes she is.

Dale: Who's here with us tonight?

Laura Lyn: Greetings, we are the children of the sun. We have come forward through the solar storms, the deep magma for the consciousness through the heat source and the masculine energy. We are delighted to dwell upon the earth core, the rich green energy. We come to inspire the human race to save the core of the earth, to stop demineralization, to attain the minerals upon the earth. We come to understand that deep energy that is salvaged and saved will protect the human race to always have enough. Our solar energy that we bring forward will help this attainment.

Mary is also here along with many children. This earth, this world is a new nursery. Many new sparks have joined us on this plane to reconcile. These sparks came from the Aborigine, the indigenous ones, the wise ones. These sparks come with a new direction and insight allowing the old wisdom to blend with the new age. They bring the old wisdom of sacrifice and preservation, the new age of discovery and inspiration, and the lighted love that is of the earth; for the Aborigines loved the green earth.

∞ The Spirit's Journey ∞

They discovered the roots deep within the earth core contain medicine that brought upon its people satisfaction, happiness, and peace. This state helped them mingle with the spirits and the spirits brought inspiration. It is now time for all those who choose to live in this lightened space to mingle.

Every person has this opportunity to allow this energy to flow through. We are now of the age where this discovery, this deep seated truth, has merged with all. And every human species, every human that is of this earth that is alive is at a time and space where they may communicate with these elders and these children. All it requires is openness, awareness, and belief.

Dale: Do you have anything else that you would like to say?

Laura Lyn: We are inspired to bring the totems through.

We understand their will be a spirit fire and the animals are blessing you with their medicine.

Dale, please study the crocodile.

Ben, please study the snake.

Rebecca, please study the Black Panther.

And Laura, please study the Elk.

Everyone: thank you.

Laura Lyn: Dale, we are here. We are delighted in your new growth and inspiration. Those chills you feel throughout your body are reminiscent of deep truths that are displayed within you. You now feel and hear the channel clearly. This is deep truth, loving and healing energy.

We thank you for working with us. We witnessed growth and through that expression we have also ascended. We will continue to work with you through spirit messages and personal insights.

Your courageousness shows through the difficult work that you have accomplished. This is a new day and you are continuing to heal beautifully. We ask that you serve to help others for in this place the growth continues. Love and honor to you.

Dale: Thank you. This is and has been an amazing journey. Thank you for your loving guidance and support. *(I was too chocked up to say: "I couldn't have done it without you.")*

Laura Lyn: There are many in the lands that are hearing the roaring of mother earth speak; the trumpets in the air of the spirit rising, the calling and the rumbles of the dead, the undead, and the unborn merging together across the world are these voices, these tones, these rumblings. People are becoming frightened or becoming aware.

The messages of the Realm to Realm passages are perfectly timed to be released for these rumblings are getting louder and people are searching.

Dale: I'd like to ask that Laura's angels and guides gently wake her and I would like to ask that you send Laura a little bit of energy or as much as you can so that she is not depleted by this process. Again I thank you.

∞ *The Spirit's Journey* ∞

∞ Realm to Realm ∞
Summary

In summary I would like to express our deepest hopes and prayers that you understand that the individual journey is never truly alone. My husband felt "locked up" and "alone" several years ago. He was imprisoned by depression and addiction. He took on a healing through his perseverance to feel and know life to its fullest. He is now shining and at a new stage of growth where he is able to speak to a few people in a setting. Along with depression and addictions he also had grueling anxiety that manifested every time he needed to talk in even the smallest of groups.

Dale is inspired to help prisoners because he understands what it feels like to be locked up . Dale was never behind bars but his mind kept him locked out of life. Dale believes in his heart many prisoners suffered as he did and possibly could find some inspiration with this book.

We are grateful to uphold this by working with a wonderful woman who works in the system, Carol Briney. Carol has offered Dale and I the opportunity to meet with prisoners and bring them books. If you feel in your heart that you would like to help bring these messages and more to the prisoners of Ohio please contact us. Donations are tax deductible through Reentry Bridge Network. Thank you from the bottom of our hearts.

Visit www.angelreader.net for more details

Laura Lyn

Many footnotes in this book are from Wikipedia. For more information on legal information please visit: http://creativecommons.org/licenses/by-sa/3.0/

Made in the USA
Lexington, KY
28 June 2012